Tucker & Me

Growing Up a Part-Time Southern Boy

Dr. Andrew J. Harvey

TO COUNCIL MEMBER-ELECT SOLTYS,
CONGRATULATIONS ON YOUR
ELECTION, AND BEST WISHES
FOR GREAT SUCCESS.

Andrew Harvey

For information, contact:

MSI Press
1760-F Airline Highway, 203
Hollister, CA 95023
Orders@MSIPress.com
Telephone/Fax: 831-886-2486

Library of Congress Control Number 2017949282

ISBN 9781942891857

Cover design by Carl Leaver

Front cover photo: Dr. Andrew Harvey

a San Juan Book

Contents

DEDICATION

This book is dedicated to my grandmother, Adeline, for the love and stability she brought to my life during my rather chaotic childhood, and to my friend Brent, without whom my young life would have been simply unimaginable.

ACKNOWLEDGEMENTS

To my wife **Davida**, my love and thanks for being my life partner, and for cheering me on chapter-by-chapter as I wrote this book. Thank you for believing in me.

To my daughter **Rachel**, thank you for all the technology help, including with the photos for this book. I hope one day you will share these stories with your children and grandchildren. Be sure to tell them that Poppy loves them.

To my great friend **Don Lacher**, you were there every step of the way in this project, and you could not have been more supportive. I hope you get to play the fire marshal in the movie.

To the people I've shared adventures with in order to create these stories, I hope I've brought them to life in the proper way. Although in some cases I may have altered your names, you can be assured I will never forget you.

To **Dr. Betty Lou Leaver**, and the great people at **MSI Press**, thank you for "getting" this project, and for believing in me as a writer. I'm proud to be part of the MSI family. Special thanks to **Carl Leaver** for the typesetting, cover design, and graphics, and to **Mary Ann Raemisch** for the editing.

To **Kenny Aronoff**, you should have your own wing in the drummers' Hall of Fame. Many thanks for the kind endorsement.

To **Andy Robinson**, actor/director extraordinaire, we've known each other for a long time, and my admiration for you is endless. Thank you for the nice endorsement of my book.

To **J. Bennett Easterling**, you wrote a great southern childhood memoir, and I thank you for the kind words you have written about my book.

To **Stacey Miller**, my longtime publicist, thanks for going on the journey with me, and for helping to get the word out about this memoir.

To **Sharon Pickrell**, of Words Done Well, thanks for your editing efforts in the earlier phases of the book.

Lastly, a tip of the hat to all the good people of Tucker, past, present, and future. I hope I've done justice to your wonderful town with this memoir. I know I will never forget Tucker, and I hope that with the publication of this book, no one else will either.

1

INTRODUCTION

Me in my big boy's suit prior
to my first plane ride to Tucker.

My first memory involves being slapped in the face. I think psychologists put some measure of meaning into your first conscious remembrance. When people who know me read about this first memory, they are probably going to say, "Okay, now that explains a lot." Well, I can't blame them for that because in many ways I feel the same.

I had just finished my lunch and was watching Sheriff John, a local Los Angeles daytime TV show for kids. I'm guessing I was only a few years old at the time because I remember still sleeping in somewhat of a crib contraption. Sheriff John was not an actual law enforcement official, but he wore a uniform that looked real to me and worked in an office that seemed pretty legitimate. However, his primary role was keeping kids like me company during lunchtime by providing good advice and playing cartoons.

In one particular cartoon, the main character, Elmer Fudd, was very bashful, particularly around female characters. When they paid attention to him, he would blush and say, "Aw, shucks." This registered with me as the appropriate thing to say when experiencing any type of female attention.

After Sheriff John was over, it was time for my nap. My mom picked me up and placed me into the bed. As mothers often do with their young children in putting them down to sleep, she stroked my face and said some loving things. I felt this was the perfect time to employ my expanded vocabulary, and so I said, "Aw, shucks." This was met with a slap in the face. Not a real hard one, but enough to send a message, which was that I was never to say those words again.

As you might imagine, this threw me for quite a loop. Certainly my trusted friend, Sheriff John, would not allow cartoons to be shown that would get a young boy into that kind of trouble. My mom had not been abusive to me that I was ever aware of, either before or after that incident. I was left alone to nap and ponder how I had come to experience this kind of humiliation, but I couldn't really come up with an answer that made any sense to me.

Looking back on this situation, now 50 years in the past, it is quite clear what happened. It can be summed up with the old movie saying from *Cool Hand Luke*: "What we've got here is failure to communicate." Although I'm still sure I said, "Aw shucks," there is no doubt what my mom heard was, "Aw, fucks," and she reacted accordingly.

Although I didn't get hit very often as a child, or spanked, as they often referred to it, I did get a bum rap on that one. I can't complain too much as there were many times when I either got off the hook altogether or had my penalty softened.

As a boy, I smacked my father very hard with a large, iron cooking spoon, dead square on the point of his elbow. He howled like a hyena, and once he recovered, he decided that corporal punishment was in order for me. As he positioned me to take the swat, my mother watched from the sidelines. As he drew his hand back, she screamed, "That's enough," and grabbed me into her arms. My father was left with the only reply possible: "I hadn't even hit him yet!" I don't know why I whacked my father with the spoon, but he probably had it coming.

When I was a little older and stronger, my dad and I were sitting in the living room of his bachelor pad, watching TV side-by-side in chairs. He accidentally knocked his drink over onto the floor. I have no idea what made him decide this, but he had the bright idea that because I would have been punished for such an infraction, he should receive sanctions as well. I'm thinking that his impaired judgment, in this case, may have had something to do with what was in the glass.

He took off his belt, gave it to me, and told me to let him have it on the backside. As was to become part of a pattern throughout my life, my father never really knew me or understood me. He thought that I would give him a little baby tap, and we'd have a good chuckle out of it.

Instead, I laid into him like there was no tomorrow, and he pleaded with me to stop. As he moved around the room to try and evade me, I gave chase, hitting him with the belt anywhere I could, with everything I had. He turned to face me, and that's when I got him right in the "tooger." Tooger was the name I had developed for my peeing equipment.

He was finally able to get the belt away from me and end the mayhem, but I have to say he looked at me in the oddest way after that. It was kind of like if having what you thought to be a little kitten turned out to be more of a wolverine. To his credit, he took his medicine like a man and did not retaliate.

My mom and dad hailed from the southern part of the country, and in the fifties, like a lot of people, they made their way out to southern California. My mom already had a son from a prior marriage when they tied the knot, and I came along in the early sixties. I was really too young to remember much about my mother and father as a couple since they divorced when I was a small boy.

My last memory of them together in the same house was one morning in the kitchen. It must have been a Monday morning because my dad was bemoaning the fact that it was "Blue Monday." I didn't know what that meant at the time, but I came to learn it was a saying to denote the third Monday in January, supposedly the gloomiest day of the year. However, I tend to think he may have meant it more generically in that the weekend was over and it was time to head back to the grind of work.

I understood my parents' marriage to be very volatile and tempestuous. As I came to know them in later years, it was hard for me to imagine them coexisting peacefully in the same home, much less the same room.

Divorce was not something that was taken lightly back then. Couples tended to tough it out and stay together even when they couldn't stand each other. A common refrain heard was that they were staying together, "for the sake of the kids." My parents could not sustain that philosophy, if they ever possessed it, and they divorced in the mid sixties when I was about 4 years old.

I think their decision ended up shaping me in many ways as I became just about the only kid in my neighborhood or school who did not have both mother and father under the same roof. This led to me, among other things, having a bit of a chip on my shoulder, which I sometimes still carry to this day. I felt that because I grew up as a boy without a father, I always had something to prove. Whether this was true or not, this perception became a furnace that powered me throughout my life to achieve, with an "I'll show you" attitude.

Making matters worse was my father's decision to remarry and move to the state of Georgia. When I learned of this, I reviewed a map of the United States. Even as a little boy, I was able to realize he could not have gotten much farther away from me unless he was going to live on a boat in the Atlantic Ocean. Knowing what I know now, he did not move thousands of miles to get away from me. He simply did what he wanted, which was to settle in the South, where he and his new wife both had family and strong roots.

Unfortunately, this was not the message that came through. This, too, added fuel to heating up that furnace. Though using such motivations can end in diverse ways I am pleased to say that I was able to channel my "male abandonment" issues in a way that yielded good results in my life. I know this is not always the case for men.

My father and his new wife settled in a small town suburb of Atlanta known as Tucker. They bought a home there, and this was to be the center of their lives for several decades. As part of the divorce agreement, my mother had primary custody of me, and I would visit my father in Georgia for one month out of the year in the summer. No one ever asked me what I thought of this arrangement. I was just told that was what was going to happen.

I went to Tucker for the first time in 1967, when I was six years old. I was taken to the airport in Los Angeles (LA), commonly known as LAX. My father would fly in from Atlanta and then fly back with me the first time. The plan was that he would exit his plane, then connect with me, and we would get on a plane bound from LA to Atlanta, and that's exactly what happened. He walked off that plane about the time our plane was due to leave, and off we went to Atlanta. When I returned to LA, I flew on my own, shepherded by the stewardesses, now called flight attendants in today's "appropriate" language.

Thus began a series of pilgrimages to Tucker that make up the heart and soul of this book. Although I might have had an interesting childhood memoir discussing only my life growing up with a single mom in the Los Angeles area, the truth of it is that what makes it unique is that I grew up living two completely separate, and very distinct, lives.

My life in Los Angeles was very different from my life in Tucker, and it wasn't easy as a little boy transitioning from one home with one way of life to another home with a different way of life every summer for about a dozen years. This book is about those transitions and the adventures that ensued.

Memoirist Mary Karr has made some interesting observations about telling one's own story. She says a memoir is the sheer, convincing poetry of a single person trying to make sense of the past, and that is, I'm sure, in part what I'm doing here.

However, I think most of it is just telling some stories that only I can tell, similar to what was done by James Herriott in my favorite book, *All Creatures Great and Small.* My stories are focused on about a 12 year time period in my young life, but they are not told necessarily in chronological order. Rather, they are simply a series of short stories that attempt to capture that time in my life. I take occasional liberty throughout the book in writing about other time periods, but primarily this is a memoir about my youth and how it shaped me.

Ms. Karr further suggests that in writing a memoir, from the second you choose one event over another, you're shaping the past's meaning. I don't doubt that for a second, but what I will tell you is that I have attempted to recount these stories for you in a completely honest and authentic way. I realize at times, as the writer, I may be a bit judgmental of the characters and their decisions, including my own actions. I certainly don't want to do that to others in an overly unkind way, and I've done my best to try and balance the writing in this regard.

Writer Tobias Wolff has said that memory has its own story to tell. This is the story of the childhood life I had, the one my memory allows me to share.

2

PLAYING WITH FIRE

At an amusement park with my dad.
Yes, that is how he dressed to go to an amusement park.

My father, George, had a rather odd love-hate relationship with fire. It reminds me of an old joke about a famous monster, which stated that Frankenstein's primary form of problem solving was strangulation. Deadly effective, but not the most subtle approach. George never strangled anyone as far as I know, but he did use fire as a key solution for vexing problems around his property.

Fire is one of those things that can be either good or bad; it all depends on the context and care in which it's put to use. George's judgment was never his strong suit, but he did have protocols he employed when using fire. Now you might think this would involve things like safety equipment, universal precautions, and the like. However, none of these cumbersome things were taken into account. There really was only one rule. When you used fire to solve a problem, you had to drink beer. A lot of it.

The first problem that emerged was an extraordinary series of nests that yellow jacket wasps had built in the front bushes at the house on Avis Lane in Tucker, Georgia. George was not really an outdoors kind of guy, so there was no telling how long their structures had remained in existence.

My friend Dale and I were often outside, and I think you know that young boys and wasps are bound to collide. This intersection of different types of life took the form of Dale getting stung on the nose. One minute he looked like Dale and the next a young W.C. Fields, the famous old-time actor known for his bulbous nose.

We immediately went into the house to lodge our complaint with George, who was hard at work in his home office as usual. I encouraged Dale to tell the story firsthand, and with the emotions and tears of a young Marlon Brando, he did just that as we were standing in the house with George listening and me watching.

As Dale was about halfway through his tale of woe, my father hauled off and slapped him in the face. Although I was certainly stunned at this, the look on Dale's face is one I wish I could have preserved for posterity. If you were going to take a picture that epitomized the term, *look of shock*, I think this would be the picture you would use.

After slapping Dale, presumably for either being stupid enough to get stung or not telling the story quickly enough, my father went into what looked like some sort of Indian rain dance, stomping on the carpet first with his right foot and then with his left as we stood by in amazement.

It was only when he stopped that we began to realize what had happened. George had seen a yellow jacket crawling onto Dale's face from behind his ear and had taken swift, affirmative action to knock it to the ground and eradicate it. Terminix®? We don't need no stinking Terminix®!

When we recovered from our shock, we knew more action would need to be taken against the attackers, but we didn't know what. My father's first move was to go into the kitchen and get a beer, which would help grease the skids of his mind. We all then went to the front yard for a reconnaissance mission, with my father in the lead, closely followed by me, and Dale very slowly bringing up the rear. After what seemed like a pretty short period of time, my father announced the strategy that would be employed: "We'll burn 'em out!"

Now you might think that such a strategy would take some time to carry out, but this was not the case. The strategy was enacted immediately by another visit to the refrigerator for a second beer, followed by a trip to the big shed under the house that held various large devices such as a riding lawn mower.

As it turns out, we had quite a bit of both gasoline and kerosene on hand. We never specifically discussed it, but I believed George thought that if one was good, the combination of the two would be better. Moreover, with regard to highly incendiary material, the old saying, "the more, the merrier," seemed to be the order of the day.

After staging all our materials in the front yard, there was only one thing to do—back to the kitchen for a third beer, and now we were ready. George had the gasoline and began pouring it generously into the front bushes. I was instructed to pour the kerosene over the gasoline. What could be better than that for a nine-year old boy? Dale watched cautiously from a distance, waiting for the kind of justice that only fire can bring.

George set fire to the bushes, and what happened next is one of those things that's difficult to describe to someone who wasn't present, but I'll do my best. If you think of a charcoal barbeque being lit after the coals have been soaked in lighter fluid, you'll get an idea—times one thousand. Initially, it was really more of an explosion than a fire, although there was definitely fire in the aftermath. I can't swear to it, but Tucker may have seen its first and only mushroom cloud that day. The wasps were incinerated, as were the bushes and anything within the area, and to this day, I'm shocked that the adjacent windows were not blown out.

How the house was not set on fire, I'll never know, but I give George some credit. By luck or choice, the house George chose to buy was brick, and those bricks stood the test on that day. I'm sure you think that as soon as the fire did its job with the wasps we immediately put out the fire with water and fire extinguishers. We would have done just that if we *had* water and fire extinguishers.

Unfortunately, with what amounted to three 9 year old boys at work, we did not have the foresight to have either present when we lit the fuse to the rocket. All's well that ends well, and the fire burned itself out quickly after the initial blaze of glory. I've never been one to confuse good luck with good tactics. That day we had good luck.

George *was* one to confuse those two concepts, and this led to our next adventure with fire the following summer. For reasons that escape me, he had, over time, collected a huge pile of garbage, brush, and tree limbs at the back of his property. Now let's see…what to do…what to do with such a thing? Oh, of course. Burn it, but only after first being properly hydrated with many beers, knocked back in a short period of time.

Dale was missing in action for this one. This was just my dad and me. We trudged down the hill of the back yard, crossed the creek, and eyed the work at hand. I don't know if the prior experience influenced him or not, or if it was just that he didn't have any kerosene on hand, but our only accelerant this time was a gallon of gasoline.

Regrettably, our prior experience had not resulted in ensuring the availability of water or fire extinguishers. In fact, the pile was so far from the house there was not even a hose line that would reach it. Such details would not deter George, though; he had a bit of a "we'll cross that bridge when we come to it" mentality.

The plan, such as it was, was for him to soak half of the pile, which formed the shape of a circle. He would then hand off the gasoline can to me, and I would finish moving around the circle, soaking it all with the gasoline until the can was empty. We would then light the bonfire, and burn, baby, burn.

As well-planned out as this all may seem, there ended up being a couple of problems. First, this pile was so high that one person standing on one side and another person standing on the other side couldn't see each other. Thus, as I poured the gasoline on the pile and moved to complete the circle, I lost sight of George.

I realized in short order this was not a good thing, as he set fire to the pile on the other side with me still pouring gasoline on my side. Why wait until the pouring of the gasoline was complete? That's crazy talk, right? As the fire took hold at lightning speed around the circle, I was blasted back by the explosive power, dropping the gasoline can onto the pile in the process. What little hair I had on my legs and arms was singed off, thus ending my ability to look like Burt Reynolds, the big, hairy movie star of the time.

Once my father knew I had almost been killed by his negligent action, he rushed to me and held me in his arms, apologizing with tears in his eyes and professing his undying love for me. Oh wait, this is a nonfiction memoir, so disregard that.

Although he did rush all right, it was to try and get the gas can out of the fire with a rake. He then chastised me for dropping the can into the fire, which gives pretty good insight into my father's capacity to properly assess culpability. Once again, with good luck, the fire burned itself out, and we trekked back up the hill to quaff a few beers, him Budweiser®, and me root.

Our final fire story involved my father's friend, Merlin, who was destined to become part of neighborhood lore for being involved in this last incident. George had already developed a reputation as a bit of an unconventional neighbor, particularly in regard to his use of fire as a form of first response to problems.

In the above instances, through sheer good fortune, things hadn't gotten out of hand. The third time wasn't the charm for my father as this incident was destined to involve the authorities, who would, no doubt, keep a closer eye on him in the future.

There was a nice creek running through the back of my father's property, and as is often the case, large brush tends to grow up on both sides of a creek. Most people would just let it grow, work to thin it out, or, perhaps, hire someone to deal with it, but George was not most people. Like a lot of problems, in his eyes, the logical solution involved fire, along with the requisite six-pack of beer to be ingested beforehand.

Enlisting Merlin to assist him in this endeavor was not overly helpful. Merlin was a very nice man, but he wasn't working in the rocket science department at NASA at that time, and he tended to go along with my father's suggestions. In this case, the suggestion was to apply gasoline all up and down each side of the creek and light it on fire. This would eliminate the pesky problem of overgrown brush. However, like a lot of things involving fire and beer, there are often unintended consequences.

George worked one side of the creek, soaking it with gasoline, and Merlin did the same on the other. You know what comes next—blast off! The neighbors on each side weren't enamored with the creek being set on fire, and they called the fire department. As the trucks arrived, my father sent Merlin up the hill to talk with them as his designated representative. George didn't know what was said between the fire captain and Merlin, but what he did know was that after the brief conversation, Merlin pointed down at him excitedly. It appeared that waterboarding was not going to be necessary to get Merlin to expose the guilty party.

After the fire personnel had ensured the whole neighborhood wasn't going to go up, the captain had a conversation with my father, to which I was not privy. Based upon his body language, though, I would venture a guess that things like "jail," "prison," "expensive fines," and "locked up for good," probably came up. At least to my knowledge, George ended his fire-starting career that day. As a result, Tucker became a much safer community to live in, albeit perhaps with fewer funny stories to tell.

3

PROBLEM CHILD

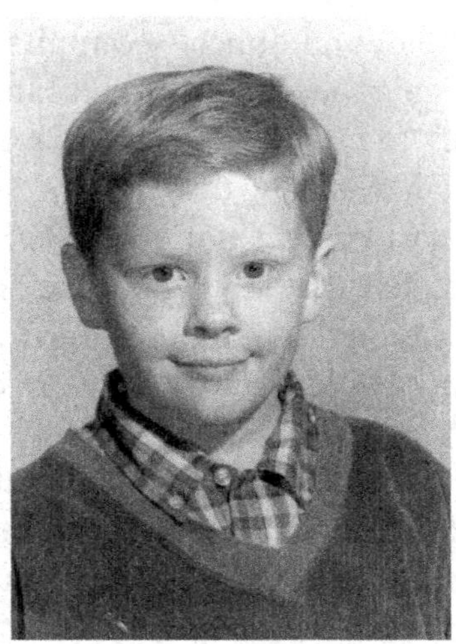

School picture.

I was born at the tail end of the Baby Boomer generation, which is usually classified as the time from 1946-1964. World War II ended in 1945, and the citizen-soldiers were coming home in droves, happy about a lot of things, not the least of which was simply being alive. Getting married and having babies, oddly enough typically done in that order, seemed to be the thing to do after surviving a war.

These were the folks dubbed "The Greatest Generation" by the Tom Brokaw book of the same name. They grew up in the Great Depression, won World War II, and built America into a world powerhouse. They were battle-tested and forged in steel.

So, how to follow an act like them? They were characterized typically by common values and a similar vision of the American dream. They believed in duty, honor, country, community, faith, family, and most of all, responsibility for oneself. This was the American fabric upon which they were woven. Oh, and they had babies—lots of them. I was one.

I was born in a hospital in the San Gabriel Valley, a loose collection of cities in a suburban area east of Los Angeles, California. A point of odd trivia: I live today on the same street as that hospital, albeit in a different city. As the story was told to me, my mother had multiple miscarriages until I finally made it out. She was 35 years old at the time—considered old to have a baby in the sixties.

As I consider my mother and father's commitment to having a child and what surely was the great heartbreak and disappointment they felt at the miscarriages, it occurs to me they must have really wanted a baby, or at least one of them did. I don't know the status of their relationship at the time I was born, but I believe it was not good. Perhaps my parents were one of those couples who felt that having a child would save, or at least improve, the marriage. Having known both of them throughout my life, my best guess is that they would have gone their separate ways at some point, regardless.

A friend of mine who knows me only as an adult is convinced that as a young boy, I must have been like the son represented in the movie *Problem Child.* For those unfamiliar with this film, the young boy had a light complexion, along with red hair, as did I as a child. The boy had adult-like characteristics, coupled with somewhat of a deviant side. He was extremely capable at outsmarting the adults, something he utterly relished doing. I think my friend may have had me pegged pretty well, despite having not known me when I was young.

I always felt like I was a small adult instead of a child. Unfortunately, with the sole exception of my brother, no one caught on to this and treated me accordingly. Instead, they acted as if I was a more typical child, which led to all kinds of problems for both them and me. I've heard people referred to as an "old soul," and I think this is how I was always wired.

A part in the movie *Ferris Buehler's Day Off* particularly resonated with me. The title character and his friends are at a very fancy restaurant in Chicago, and he is being treated with disdain by the very snooty maître d'. As Ferris locks horns with this individual, his friend says that he should be careful because they might get busted.

Ferris then turns and speaks to the camera, thus addressing the audience directly. He says he doesn't "get busted." However, if he were going to get busted, it most certainly would not be by a guy like the maître d'. I feel similarly now in my life, but looking back, that is also how I felt as a child. Stories from my childhood, shared here, should show the kind of kid I was.

I remember in fifth grade we had a teacher's aide named Miss Johnson. I didn't really know what a teacher's aide was at the time, but it seems to me now the young lady was what you might call a teacher-in-training. Spending time in the classroom with an experienced teacher would springboard her to her own teaching opportunity, but first, she would have to cross swords with the "problem child."

I was never a cheater at any point in my academic career. I always did my own work and never plagiarized. However, as a result of my being framed for some hijinks in class, Miss Johnson decided I needed to be punished. We were studying geology at the time, so she assigned me a one-page paper as a punitive sanction. I felt this was wholly unfair and began to consider my options.

I ultimately decided not to write the paper but to copy it straight from the encyclopedia we had at home, which conveniently differed from the encyclopedia available at the school. This was long before the Internet, which makes catching cheating easy. I felt my approach was a fair compromise in that it would get the teacher off my back, but I would have the satisfaction of not actually having been "punished" by being forced to create an original paper.

After copying the entry on geology from the encyclopedia, it occurred to me that there were various words used that were not common in the lexicon of young boys, words like *gorge* and *chasm*. I anticipated that Miss Johnson would be suspicious of my high-level writing and would attempt to catch me by having me define the words I used in the paper. If I couldn't define the words I used, I would look like a fool and a cheater, and would, no doubt, get a more severe punishment. So, I made sure I knew the dictionary definition of each word that might be considered an unusual word-choice by a fifth grader.

I turned in my paper the next day, and Miss Johnson called me to her desk fairly soon thereafter. She asked me to define the exact words I had predicted she would ask me. I had these words down cold. After giving her the first definition she was taken aback, but she pressed on through the second and third, which I also nailed.

By this point, she was clearly losing steam as the result of my *Jeopardy* champion-like performance. She made one more feeble attempt, which I crushed into the ground. Her face showed she knew she was beaten at this point. Miss Johnson rose up in her chair with as much dignity as she could muster and said simply, "You can return to your seat now, Andy."

I take almost as much glee now in telling this story as I did in living it some 45 years ago. Miss Johnson, if you're reading this, it was not personal, but as with Ferris Buehler, I was simply not going to get busted, and if I were going to get busted, it wasn't going to be by someone who was just learning how to teach. This encounter reinforced a belief I had even as a child and carry with me to this day: I may not always win, but I will always be the one who is most-prepared.

In that same grade, toward the end of the year, we had games and festivities, one of which involved guessing the amount of candy in a very large jar. Whoever guessed the right amount of individual candies was the winner. I didn't care about the candy, but I did care about winning, as I was wired to be extraordinarily competitive, something that was often discouraged by my teachers who would classify my displeasure at losing as being a "poor sport." In essence, they were trying to filter out of me the exact quality that would help me be successful in life—thanks a lot.

In any event, I watched as other children tried futilely to maintain their count of the giant candy jar. I had other ideas. When there was no activity around the jar, I took a ruler and decided that I would focus my efforts on counting the candies in exactly one inch of the jar. This would not necessarily give me an accurate count, but I believed it would give me a better chance to focus with precision on a small area, and then multiply that area by the total height of the jar, which was cylindrical.

I submitted my guess, and what do you know, I was right on the money! However, some other smarty-pants student named Lauren was also right on the money, so a tie-breaker had to be employed between her and me. The teacher decided that a student's mother who was helping out in class would select a number from one to one hundred. Each of us would pick a number, and the one closest to the number she picked would win. I was to go first.

By going first, I was limited, in that if I picked any number too high or too low, my opposition could simply pick the next number up or down and have the odds in her favor. I believed the mother would select a number that was either her age, or close to it, and I believed her to be in her forties. I chose the number 49, hoping to bait Lauren into picking 50, thus giving me half of the numbers, and in particular all of the forties. I was astonished when she picked 67. How could anybody be so foolish to pick such a number? Why not pick the number 50?

As it turns out, the number was 43, within the range I had imagined, and I was declared the winner. This experience also taught me something. Lauren was no dummy. In fact, she was quite smart. We once were doing a play in which she was one of the leads. On the first day of rehearsal, everyone was reading from the script, but not Lauren. She had already memorized all of her lines and was able to recite them without looking at the script. I was most impressed with this because she was clearly obsessed with preparation as the key to success, just as I had learned with Miss Johnson. That is why, many years later in life, I asked Lauren to marry me. Oh, wait, I'm just kidding about that part!

Although Lauren was smart and willing to work hard to prepare, she was not strategic. I learned that day that being smart and well-prepared is not enough. You must also be strategic in your thinking, something that I have carried forward. People have often described me as calculating, and my guess is that sometimes they mean it in a complimentary fashion, and other times not, but for better or worse, this seems to be how I am wired.

My calculating behavior applied to sports as well. Typically only certain grades of kids were out on the playground at a given moment, but there was one time of day where everyone from first grade to eighth grade was outside. That was in the morning before the first bell rang. There were games of kickball and the like where you might have 20 people roaming the outfield in all age groups.

As you might imagine, the older kids dominated. If somehow a young one managed to get "up" to kick, he would usually kick the ball in somewhat of a bunting style and be out before he had taken two steps to first base as the other kids swarmed toward home plate just as he was about to kick.

One day when I was in perhaps second grade, I caught such a bunt-like kick and had my chance to kick—not a common occurrence for someone in that age group. Under no circumstances was I going to do a bunt kick. The kids must've somehow sensed this because they didn't dare crowd in at home plate. There must have been something about my body language. In any event, skilled or not, I didn't have the same capacity as kids who were in some cases twice my age so I knew I needed to have a game plan if I were to be successful.

I noticed an older boy at first base. He was nicknamed "The Dough-boy" because he had somewhat of a Michelin-Man® physique. I didn't suspect he was known for his defense so he became my target. I also saw that if I managed to launch the ball over the Doughboy's head, there would be no one behind him in that area and the ball would roll until it couldn't roll anymore.

I kicked it with everything I had, and the ball bee-lined to Doughboy. He was in shock that I'd done this, but he did manage to put his arms in the air. Jumping was, of course, out of the question. I can still remember the look on the Doughboy's face when the ball cleared his outstretched fingers. I was then able to go into a rather casual home-run trot as there was no chance of anyone retrieving the ball anytime soon.

The looks on the older boys' faces were priceless. They stared open-jawed as I "touched 'em all." I placed the ball in the only location where I would've had even a remote chance of a home run. This is the kind of approach I've tried to employ my whole life.

A good example of how I applied strategic thinking in later years is the story of how I acquired my first girlfriend in high school. At the time, I lived in the relatively small town of South Pasadena, a suburb of Los Angeles. I was most fortunate to drive a flashy sports car, a red Corvette.

I usually had the top down so I had great visibility from inside the car. People could also see me quite well as I sat in the open vehicle.

As I was driving around during the summer, on a few occasions I noticed a cute girl walking by herself. Each time, we made eye contact and smiled a bit, and I gave myself a stern pep talk to stop and attempt to chat her up or even offer her a ride the next time I saw her. My ways with girls at the time involved words that started with a "p." You must be thinking now of words like *powerful* and *persuasive*. The more accurate "p-words" at that time, though, would have been more like *pathetic* and *pitiful*. Nonetheless, I steeled myself for our next encounter.

Naturally, at this point, I didn't see her again. Further, I did not recognize her from high school. In that school district, high school started at the sophomore year, and junior high extended all the way up to ninth grade, which would typically be the freshman year of high school. I guessed that she might have been an incoming sophomore.

I went to my old junior high school yearbook and pored over it with military precision. Sure enough, I spotted her. My theory was correct. She would be a sophomore that year. This would make her a "younger woman" for me, but not by much. Her name was Donna.

Back in those days, phonebooks were quite popular, and many people had what was known as a "listed" number. Based on her somewhat unusual last name, I found a listing that I believed to be for her mother. I summoned up what was at that point the maximum amount of courage I possessed and called the number, only after endless internal debate and stalling. I called on a summer weekday, hoping her mom would be at work. Luck was with me, and Donna answered the phone.

In my smoothest delivery, which was a laugh to say the least, I said hello and told her my name. I asked her if she remembered seeing the guy in the red Corvette, and she said she did. I told her that was me, and she seemed quite surprised by this call out-of-the-blue, yet pleasantly so. I asked if she would like to go out with me sometime, and she readily agreed. We chose a day and time when I would come over to get her, and we hung up. Now it was my turn to be surprised—surprised that I had actually pulled off this outrageous plan.

Pick her up I did, and we went for the traditional dinner and a movie. She was a real doll, fun and sweet-natured. We enjoyed the summer by driving around and doing all kinds of silly things. I particularly remember watching some Dodgers' games and enjoying some spirited rounds of miniature golf. We were both pretty innocent.

When it was time for her family to go to the beach for their summer vacation, she invited me down to spend the day with her. It was a great time, one I'll always remember. We ended up by ourselves in the family's hotel room, with just me and her on the bed, and yes, we were fully-clothed. I remember the radio being on and the beautiful love song, "The Closer I Get to You" by Roberta Flack and Donny Hathaway, coming on. Even to this day, almost 40 years later, that song immediately transports me back to that moment.

We heard the key insert in the hotel room door, and we popped up out of that bed as if we had been shot out of a cannon. It was her mom, who didn't make a fuss about it—I think because we had all of our clothes on. We both said in unison, "Nothing" before she was even able to pose the classic question, "What were you doing?"

Alas, our romance ended sooner than I would have liked. We remained good friends through high school and even as young adults. She was a great first girlfriend for me, and that relationship gave me a boost of confidence that I was in real need of at the time. No matter how long I live, she will always be my first…kiss. Donna, if you're reading this, I hope you remember those times as fondly as I do.

In this chapter, I've tried to give you an "at a glance" look at who I was as a boy. Overall, I was a good kid, but very physical in nature and a strategic thinker. In the end, I guess some of the other kids and adults I encountered would have labeled me as the "Problem Child," as my friend did many decades later.

4

RIDING THE WILD MATTRESS

On the staircase where the wild mattresses were ridden.

I was a planned Cesarean birth. The doctor gave my mother a choice of several dates for delivery, and she picked the 17th. This was because her birthday was on the 17th, albeit in a different month. This was part of an inordinate role the number 17 played in our family.

I was brought home as a baby to our residence in the Los Angeles suburb of Monterey Park. I only lived there until I was two years old, but it was always referred to as the Hermosa Vista House, in reference to the name of the street. The street number was 417, thus continuing an odd streak of the number 17 in our family residences.

Prior to that house, my family lived in the city of Alhambra, with a street address of 1717. The next home we moved to, the address was simply 17. Ultimately, the family settled in another town, where the house number was 1728. That's an awful lot of 17s for one family.

The first home I remember was on Los Higos Street in the city of Alhambra, another Los Angeles suburb, where I lived from the time I was two until I became a teenager. I loved that home, it was perhaps one of the most unique houses I've ever encountered. It was a two-story brick home that was built in 1935 by a contractor as his personal residence. At the time it was built, it was the only house on the block, and it was situated among an enormous colony of orange groves.

The home formally faced a north/south street, but over the years a long driveway was built on the east/west cross street, and that was where we typically entered and exited the property. Other homes were eventually built up around this house, which was located pretty far from the adjacent streets. We had what is known as an "easement" on the eastside of the property. This area ultimately became the driveway of another home, but the easement allowed us to legally access the driveway as a walkway to get to and from our house.

The neighbors at that house in front were not fond of the easement and would stare at us when we strolled down their driveway to our home. There's a thing about easements that you should know. In order to maintain your legal right to traverse the land, you must use it regularly. If you didn't, the neighbors could claim that you had lost your right to move through their property. In other words, use it or lose it.

My mom was somewhat obsessed with the easement, using it whenever she could and insisting that we do likewise. She would regularly announce that we must use the easement more often in order to preserve our legal standing. This standing was never actually challenged, but who knows, maybe that was because of my mother's diligence in maintaining it.

One of the unique features of the house was that the upstairs and downstairs were self-contained, in that there was a bedroom, a bathroom, a kitchen, and much living space on each floor. There were two separate staircases, one indoors and one outdoors. Thus, two separate families could live quite comfortably there, one on the top and one on the bottom.

The interior staircase was the venue for what became one of the signature activities of the home. It was called "Riding the Wild Mattress." Now I know what you're thinking, and no, it was not that. The inside staircase was very wide and carpeted. I don't remember how it came to be, but at some point, I came up with a plan. The idea was to take a single-sized mattress, place it at the top of the stairs, and ride it down to the bottom, sort of like a magic carpet.

One of the key challenges of this ride was that there was a solid brick wall at the end of the staircase. After a few incidents in which there were some crash landings, it was decided among my fellow mattress-riders that we would actually need two mattresses—one to ride, and another propped up to cushion the brick wall at the landing.

There were various experiments that went on with my friends and other kids in the extended family, but ultimately it was determined that in order to optimize the ride's effect, we needed to do certain things. First, we placed a slick, satin-style fitted sheet on the bottom of the mattress to create a faster glide. We learned to limit it to two riders at a time, with at least one "pusher," who would enhance the natural speed of gravity by taking a running start and propelling the mattress and riders down the stairs.

We would do this endlessly, and with the energy of youth, we never seemed to get tired. We did not have the ability to clock our speed with a radar gun, but I feel pretty confident in saying we got up to speeds far faster than any sane parent would have allowed.

Decades later, I ran into a friend who had taken part in this homemade amusement park ride. Literally the first thing he said to me was, "Ride the Wild Mattress!" This was one ride that created a long-lasting imprint, and I'm kind of glad there was no one else within earshot when he greeted me with this phrase.

I remember my father being around during the very early parts of our living in this house, but he ultimately moved on and ended up in Tucker. Thus, my formative years were spent in this house primarily with my mom. Being a single mother back then was unusual. All of my friends had both their mother and father at home. Unlike today when being a single mother has evolved into somewhat of a badge of honor, being a single mother in the sixties carried a stigma.

I grew up in that house and went to Baldwin elementary school for kindergarten through eighth grade, where I got a fine education and had a heck of a good time. My mother went through a series of transitory relationships, two of them culminating in marriage. It seemed that my mom would use marriage as a form of dating. Most people would date first and then, if things went well, get married. My mom tended to get married first and then go through the dating process to determine if it was, in fact, a good match.

There was Gabe, a Hispanic man who was quite nice to me. He spoke Spanish and was teaching me how to count in that language during the time he and my mom were married. I only made it up to 40, which should give you a pretty good indication of how long that marriage lasted. My one regret about Gabe going on his way was that if he had stood the test of time, I would have no doubt been fluent in Spanish by now, which would have been great.

Then there was Bobby the Butcher, so named because he was, well, a butcher. My mother had been dating him for only a short while when they announced they would be taking a little trip together. I was to stay with my beloved grandmother so I really didn't think much about it.

When they returned from this journey, we all stood in the large master bedroom while they were telling me about the trip. My mom said we should all go into the closet because she wanted to tell me something. Now mind you, this was a large walk-in closet. I didn't understand why we should go in there to talk, but go in there we did. The three of us held hands, and my mom told me that they had gotten married on the trip, which I learned later was a trip to Las Vegas, and that Bobby was to be my new father. I never found out why we went into the closet to announce the big news, and I wish now I had asked.

So, a few problems here. First, even as a young child, I knew that it was foolish to get married after having known each other such a short time. Second, it sure would have been nice if my mom had solicited my feelings about making such a move prior to doing so. Third, I didn't like surprises then, and I don't like them now, particularly surprises of this nature. My reaction was to throw myself on the bed and yell, "Oh, no!" The irony of this was that it wasn't long before my mom was doing that same thing in response to the marriage.

That closet was also the home of my mother's furs. Back in those days, women regularly wore actual animal furs without getting chastised and splashed with paint. My mom even had a mink stole, which I will describe for you, even though it will be hard for younger readers to believe me. A mink is a small, furry animal slaughtered to make into clothing, but the head and the legs were left intact. Thus, it was just as if you were wearing an actual dead animal.

Typically, three of these minks would be used to complete the mink stole. The one part of the animal that was removed was the teeth, and a clipping device was inserted into the mouth. This allowed you to clip multiple minks together by attaching the mouth of one mink to the tail of the next one, thus shaping an oval that would then be worn around a woman's neck. This was, indeed, considered high-style back in the day.

We had a very sweet-natured dog named Mopsie at the time. Every once in a while, when I was left unsupervised in the house, which was a lot, I would take out one of my mom's minks from a drawer in the closet. I know you must be thinking that I had some kind of fetish, but not so. It was simply a creative device I used to create a fun game of chase with my dog. First, you must realize that Mopsie did not have an understanding that the mink was long dead. To her, this was a living interloper to be despised and, if possible, destroyed.

As I ran around the house with the mink held high in my hands, Mopsie was right behind me in hot pursuit. She would jump as high as she could and at the apex of the jump would snap her jaws shut in an attempt to bag the mink. I would run up and down the stairs, leap over the chaise lounge, hop onto the bed, and engage in every other acrobatic and evasive maneuver I could think of, with Mopsie barking relentlessly, always right on my heels no matter the obstacle.

She was utterly furious at the audacity of this mink, thinking it could show itself without suffering grievous sanctions. It is probably best for both Mopsie and me she never got hold of the mink because she would have torn it to shreds. These furs were expensive, and I wouldn't have wanted to explain that one to the insurance company representative. She could not stand the animal that lived in that drawer in the closet.

As with Gabe, Bobby was also quite nice to me, but there was one main problem: he was a drunk, and a nasty one at that. Further exacerbating this situation was the fact that Bobby was about 6' 4" and 230 pounds. So, to recap, a mean drunk that size who was highly skilled in the use of knives and cleavers—what could go wrong? This is without even getting into his rifle and shotgun collection stored in the closet. Luckily, the marriage to Bobby ended before he could kill us, but there were, shall we say, some "incidents."

In one case, Bobby had failed to come home on time. We had learned that when this happened, he was typically not out collecting for the Red Cross. Rather, he was delayed as the result of being "thirsty." We watched from the second story window as he finally arrived in his car. He walked toward the back steps, and my mom remarked, "He's crawling!" As a young child, I didn't fully understand this because he appeared to me to be walking rather than crawling, but my mom insisted he was crawling.

As we moved toward the back door where Bobby was to enter, there was a very large crash, and even without seeing what caused it, it was pretty clear to both of us that Bobby had felt, at least for that night, that breaking down the door would be a better alternative than going to all the trouble of turning the door knob.

My mom and I weren't going to wait around to see what Bobby's intentions were. We hightailed it down the opposite stairway from the one Bobby had used. Now, there were two ways we could flee at this point, either down the long driveway or via the easement. You guessed it, we headed for the easement. It was nice to know that as we ran for our lives from Bobby the Butcher, we were also actively engaging our legal right to traverse our neighbor's driveway, thus preserving our easement.

We ended up two blocks away at an older couple's home. They were kind enough to take us in and let us call the authorities. We later met the police back at the house. Bobby was still there, albeit in much more contrite form. As was typical with the police in those days for domestic situations, they told Bobby to leave for the night and if they had to come back they would kick his ass *and* take him to jail. Bobby chose the option of leaving and not returning that night.

I recall my mom and Bobby divorcing shortly after that. I liked Bobby and thought he was a pretty good guy, except when he was drunk, and that was a lot of the time. I guess it would be somewhat like saying a car was really good, except that it didn't have an engine; definitely a fatal flaw.

About the only time Bobby and I would clash was when I would "dispute his word." This meant whenever I questioned anything he said or indicated that what he was saying was not accurate. I literally asked him, "You mean whenever you are obviously wrong, I'm not supposed to mention it?"

He said, "That's right."

"What about if I see you're going to make a big mistake? Am I still not to speak up and tell you you're wrong and are headed for disaster?"

He said, "That's right."

Well, there's not much you can say to such a person so I tried not to dispute his word even when his words were wrong and, often in Bobby's case, slurred. I can't end this part about Bobby without telling the story of how I found out that he slept in the nude.

My mom and Bobby had their bedroom on the second floor, and I had my room on the first floor. To that point in my young life, even having lived in California for all of my first ten years, I had not experienced an earthquake. Early one morning while we were all still asleep, the earthquake decided it was time. Having lived through many earthquakes since then, my memory of it is as the worst I've ever felt. Further complicating matters was the fact that I wasn't really sure what it was, but I knew it wasn't good.

I jumped out of bed and headed toward the bottom of the stairs. I had not made a decision yet whether I was going to run outside or head up the stairs to my mom when I saw him. An image that will, as FDR once said, "live in infamy." As I looked up to the top of the stairs, there was Bobby the Butcher, standing there in all his naked glory, and he was motioning me to come up to him. I flew up the stairs, perhaps even faster than we went down while riding the wild mattress.

Looking back on it, I realize that my mom's initial reaction was to scream my name, at which point Bobby, bless his heart, took off to fetch me. Truth be told, I would have been much safer exiting the door next to the stairs and getting outside instead of heading upstairs, but everybody's heart was in the right place on that long-ago morning, so I'm at peace with it. However, the sight of Bobby the Butcher standing at the top of the stairs is an image that will never leave me. Between the wild mattress rides and the earthquake incident, this particular staircase was a pretty big part of my memories of that house.

I really loved growing up in that home. Other than the possible exception of the house I've lived in as an adult for the past almost 30 years, it is my favorite home. When I graduated from eighth grade, it was time for me to move on to high school. My mother was concerned about some of the emerging gang influences in that area so she made a decision for us to move to another local community for my high school years. The plan was for us to rent an apartment during those years, lease our house, and then return to live in our home after I graduated from high school four years later.

When we made the move to the new apartment, my mom's furs made the move with us, but sadly, Mopsie did not. It turns out the apartment allowed dead animals but not live ones. My mother was not very specific about how Mopsie was dispositioned but alluded to finding a good situation for her. Knowing my mom as I do, my money would be on an ending for Mopsie that was not so good.

I thought then, and I still think now, that it was a lame-brained idea. As usual, nobody asked me what I thought of the plan. Rather, I returned from my annual trek to Tucker, and when we pulled into the driveway, I saw a real estate sign. That was my first inkling that I would no longer be living in the only home I had ever known. When I saw that sign, I maxed out on every obscenity I had in my teenage vocabulary, which even then was fairly substantial.

Worse, about a year into this 4 year plan, my mom sold our home for a song, that song being $50,000. Again, I was not consulted, and again, I thought it was a terrible, half-baked idea. Since my brother and I were the only two siblings, there was always an unspoken understanding that one day we would inherit the house and live there, each with our own separate living quarters yet together as brothers on the same property. There would not have even been a fight over the upstairs versus the downstairs. I liked the top floor, and he liked the bottom floor best.

About eight years later, the house was sold again for—wait for it—$750,000. How could it have gone up so much in such a relatively short amount of time? Well, that's southern California real estate for starters, but the real key was that the lot was designated as an "R-3." This meant approval to build multi-family housing on it was already in existence. You might think maybe my mom didn't know this, but no, she knew it and spoke of it often over the years.

The fact that I was proven right in my thinking about this house was not much consolation. The saddest thing of all? The house was, in fact, bulldozed to make way for condominiums. You got that? Condos!

There is a classic short film made by Laurel and Hardy called *The Music Box*. In this movie, the boys attempt to move a piano up a very long and daunting outdoor staircase. Although the film was made in 1929, the actual staircase is still there, and I have visited it a few times. At the bottom of the stairs, there is a historical marker from the City of Los Angeles commemorating the site.

If I had my way, there would be a historical sign placed where my old house was to indicate the location where the wild mattresses were first ridden. I think of that house quite often, and I believe I always will.

5

LIFE IN TUCKER

At bat in the Tucker neighborhood.

My life in Los Angeles with my mother and various stepfathers was mundane most of the time. I would get up, go to school, come home, have dinner, do my homework, and watch some television. The next day was rinse and repeat. There were also the weekends, but we really didn't go anywhere or do anything.

Complicating matters, my mom refused to drive on the freeways because they were "not safe," statistics to the contrary be damned. However, she may have been right. With her driving on the freeways, they would've been unsafe. I was pretty much left to my own devices to entertain myself.

During the summer, it was about the same, with one exception. I stayed home by myself while my mother went to work. Leaving little boys home unattended for ten hours a day might not have been the best strategy, but that's what happened. Making matters worse, my friends from school lived all the way on the other side of town. Usually, in the month of July, I headed to Tucker, and that is where my daily schedule and routine changed dramatically.

Typical days in Tucker, no matter the day of the week, were pretty consistent, but life there was vastly different from my Los Angeles schedule. We would get up between nine and ten a.m. I usually woke up to the sound of my father working from his home office in the living room. Since he ran his own business from home and never really had to "be" at work, he set his own schedule.

About four days a week we would have breakfast at home. Breakfast consisted of Hungry Jack® biscuits with butter, along with bacon, ham, and sausage. Now, you probably thought I meant bacon, ham, *or* sausage, but it was right the first time. Yes, we had bacon, ham, *and* sausage to go with the biscuits and butter. Again, you might be thinking we had this kind of lavish and heavy breakfast once in a while. Nope, when we had breakfast at home, this is what we had every time. The adults would wash it down with coffee, and I would have milk or orange juice.

About three days a week we would go out to breakfast, and this was one of the most difficult decisions of the day. So many great southern restaurants to choose from for breakfast, right? Well, whenever we went out to breakfast, it was to the Waffle House®. I'm talking about every single time, over the course of the twelve years or so I was there for the summer.

The Waffle House® is a southern tradition. First started in 1955, ironically in the Tucker area, it offers quick and easy diner food. It's not where you go for fine dining, but you won't leave hungry. As you might imagine, they loved the Waffle House®, and me, well as I said, when I left I wasn't hungry anymore. One thing I can promise you, though, is that in all the years I visited Tucker, I was never once asked where I would like to go to breakfast, or for any other meal for that matter.

So, where did the difficult decision arise if we always went to the Waffle House®? Well, you see, there were three of them within a similar distance in and around Tucker. Agonizing discussions would be held about *which* Waffle House® to go to. Arguments were made, pros and cons assessed, schedules of favorite waitresses taken into account: "Katy doesn't work on Wednesdays!"

Eventually, we would head off, with my father at the wheel of the Cadillac. Never once did I ever see his wife, Pauline, drive with him as the passenger. The man drove in every family I knew of, and I think it might be one of the very few traditions that has actually stood the test of time to this day.

In those days, you might even hear men refer disparagingly to "women drivers." Now, any man making such a comment, jokingly or not, would have their career and reputation ruined, and they would be apologizing with a *mea culpa* a day for six months straight, along with being forced to undergo extensive sensitivity training to neuter their misogynistic tendencies. Times were different then in many, many ways.

Once we finally arrived at the diner, it was time to order. There was a little more variation in the food from our breakfast at home, but not much. I should also say that the salt shaker was in high demand during all of our meals. You certainly wouldn't want to have bacon without adding a substantial amount of salt to it.

Another advantage to this restaurant was that although we were normally there at breakfast time, you could get breakfast food all day long, and all day long meant 24 hours a day. Occasionally we would go for bacon and eggs in the evening after having bacon and eggs in the morning.

One meal my father liked to order was hamburger steak smothered in onions. Like a lot of little boys, there were times when I would copy what my father ordered. Katy was one of our favorite waitresses, and one year I ordered this dish, just like my father. The next year I came back, and we visited this Waffle House® again. When Katy came to take our order, she addressed me first by asking if I wanted "the usual." I asked her what she meant, and she said, "You know, hamburger steak smothered in onions."

I was impressed with this as I had not eaten there for a year so I have to tip my hat to Katy on that one. By the way, the Waffle House® is still going strong. There are presently four in Tucker alone. Imagine the decisions about which one to go to with four of them in just that community.

My father typically ordered his meat well done. We regularly ate steak, and especially prime rib. I ordered mine well done because that was what he did. I didn't really have any experience with eating out, and when my mom made a steak, she certainly didn't ask me how I wished it to be prepared. As I learned in later years, she also cooked things to well done standards, so I really didn't know any better.

When I was an adult, I was able to figure out that I didn't really like things well done, and I began ordering my steaks medium. This was only after requesting them to a specification that was actually not my preference for many years. In fact, in later years when my mom was cooking a piece of meat, I would tell her to take mine off the grill when she thought it was about five minutes away from being done.

After returning from breakfast in the late morning, my father would go back to the home office and work, Pauline would fiddle around with things in the house, and I would be told to go out and play. Well, it's not like they took me around the neighborhood and showed me around so I had to fend for myself. This is where my experience living in LA was actually helpful.

I got to know the neighborhood kids, who were a pretty good bunch. I believe they actually looked forward to my arrivals in July to spice things up, in particular, my best buddy Dale, who earned a chapter all his own in this book. We would play all kinds of outside activities and games, usually for the entire afternoon.

Once the day's games were concluded, it was time for dinner. We almost always ate out at a restaurant. Maybe once a month Pauline would make a homemade dinner, which was actually pretty good. We would have all kinds of southern favorites like country ham, yams, fried okra, mashed potatoes, and cornbread. On very rare occasions when we would have people over, my father would barbecue, and we would have homemade ice cream.

We ate out at some pretty good places. So much so that on one of my Tucker trips, I gained 30 pounds. You heard right, 30 pounds in a month. That amount of weight gain accrued, despite the enormous amount of activity I was engaging in during the day outside in the summer heat.

When I returned to LA, my mom said we were going to go to a "special doctor." This special doctor seemed very interested in what I ate and what my activity levels were.

More often than not, we would return home after dinner in Tucker, but periodically we would go to the movies, or as my father would say, "goat the show." We saw quite a few movies, some memorable, others not so memorable. Two that stand out are *Walking Tall* and *Blazing Saddles.*

Walking Tall was based on the true-life adventures of Sheriff Buford Pusser in McNairy County, Tennessee. Joe Don Baker was sensationally powerful as the sheriff who risked everything to clean up the corruption after returning to his hometown. Many years later, an actor friend of mine told me great stories about working with Joe Don Baker, but, alas, those will have to remain private. Suffice it to say, he was a larger-than-life character both on and off screen.

This movie was also of interest to my family because my mom and her relations hailed from, you guessed it, McNairy County, Tennessee. There was a more recent remake of this movie starring the actor, The Rock, but I remain a devotee of the original.

Blazing Saddles was an outrageous spoof of westerns made by Mel Brooks. One of the most famous parts of that movie was the campfire scene where the cowboys, who had been eating copious amounts of beans, began doing what cowboys who eat copious amounts of beans do. The entire audience was busting up, but I particularly remember my father was doubled over in laughter, as was I. We made eye contact, and it was a nice moment I'll always remember.

Dale told me that his father had also enjoyed the movie, in particular when ex-football player Alex Karras, as Mongo, literally decked the horse of a guy who had mouthed off to him. Making it even funnier was that the guy was on the horse when Mongo decked it. This movie could never be made today due to the outrageous racial language and stereotypes, but it went over big in the South in that era.

The other thing we enjoyed was Putt-Putt golf. This was a miniature golf place with three eighteen-hole courses, which stayed open literally all night. Now, this was not like the golf courses you're thinking of, with windmills and such. Rather, this was a more straightforward setup that was, in essence, a series of putting greens. George and Pauline loved Putt-Putt, and I did, too. We typically ate dinner quite late and then hit the links, where we would play all three courses. It was not uncommon for us to be out there at one or two in the morning.

I remember ordering a trick golf ball from the Johnson Novelty Company. This ball was slightly bigger on one side than the other, thus causing it to never roll in a straight line. However, it was only upon very close examination of this ball that you could detect this discrepancy. I got old George pretty good one night with this ball. Every shot he hit would start out straight toward the hole but then veer off either left or right. I'm not sure how long it would have taken him to catch on, but I think it was my laughing that gave it away.

If I recall correctly, the best score I ever got was a 33 for an 18 hole course, which was pretty good. I remember sometime later, after coming back home to LA, receiving a golf scorecard which purported that Pauline had scored a 32, beating my all-time score by one. Whether it was a setup or not, I don't know. She was pretty good at Putt-Putt, so sadly, I cannot rule out that it was legitimate. Knowing all the players, however, I also can't rule out that it was a setup.

You don't normally see a 7 year old boy out on the Putt-Putt courses at two a.m., but that was just how we rolled in Tucker. After arriving home, we would watch The Big Movie, which was typically some old black-and-white film that *started* between one and two in the morning. We would all fall asleep on the couch or a chair in the TV area during this movie. At some point we would wake up and stagger off to bed, usually on an individual basis. I don't believe anyone actually ever made it all the way through The Big Movie.

So you see, my life in Tucker was quite dramatically different from my life in LA and quite distinct as well from that of a typical young man. I guess it wouldn't be a memoir worth reading if that wasn't the case. For all the craziness of it, I still have some good memories from those days. I do hope to get back to the South one day, play some Putt-Putt, and return to the Waffle House®. I don't know if Katy still works there, but if she does, I'm expecting she'll ask me if I'd like the usual, and I just might.

6

TRIXIE JO

One of my mom's famous silhouette photos.

My mother was from the South, and she retained that southern charm throughout her life, but she was a bit inconsistent in displaying it. She was a complicated figure, who ran the gamut from sweet southern lady to hell-on-wheels bully. I guess we all have different sides to us, but I think my mom may have been more extreme in each direction than most.

Her given name was Beatrice, but when she was a little girl, for some reason they started calling her Trixie Jo. The name stuck, and she was known to everyone throughout her life as Jo. She was a depression-era baby and grew up very poor. I think living during such periods has a lifetime impact on people. Most are influenced to become very thrifty in their spending, even as they become wealthy in later life. My mom had the opposite reaction, spending what she had, plus some, before someone could take it away.

Mom was a young girl when World War II came, and like many in that generation, the war affected her greatly. She had a distaste for Japanese people after the Pearl Harbor attack, and this never left her. In today's politically correct times, people would be quick to classify my mom as racist. It is interesting to note that the people who would typically do that have never lived through a world war, not knowing whether their country would still exist at the end.

It is easy now, when our nation is not under imminent threat of takeover, to navel gaze and pontificate. Perhaps not so easy during those periods. I feel it best to judge a person by the standards of their time, rather than in the more "enlightened" period we live in now—a period which they knew nothing about when they lived. Hopefully, future generations will make their judgements of us in this way, rather than holding us to some standard that emerges after we are gone.

My mom was married six times during her lifetime. Well, six that I know of anyway. She was notorious for engaging in revisionist history, either not bringing up certain people or situations or altering the story greatly to suit the image she wished to portray. One of my favorite examples was in her actions with pictures.

In those days, there were no digital pictures. They were all printed out at the local photo shop or drugstore, and you kept them in a shoebox. Whenever my mom ended a relationship with someone, be it romantic or otherwise, one of the first things she would do is go to the picture box and cut that person out of all the pictures.

You're probably thinking that she would cut them in half to eliminate the offending person. Nope, not my mom. She would literally cut them out of the picture in silhouette fashion. You could clearly see a person was sitting there, who had been surgically removed. I still possess some of those pictures.

My mom's first marriage was to Gene, my brother's father, a man who was killed in the Korean War. This expanded her anger beyond the Japanese to the Koreans and perhaps simply to Asians in general. Obviously, this was a horrible thing for my mom to endure. She became a "war widow." I thought her next marriage was to my father, but I learned in later years there was a brief marriage in between. My mom never spoke of this, and I only learned of it through unusual circumstances.

The marriage to my father lasted a while but was very tempestuous. There were reportedly instances of domestic violence. I don't doubt this, as my parents were two people in the oil-and-water category. Somehow, they stayed together long enough to have me, which was a good thing. Otherwise you would not have this memoir to read.

Mom continued on the matrimony path, marrying a few others. These were, for the most part, relatively short marriages that were never meant to be. My mom was a very impulsive and impetuous person, and this certainly applied to making decisions about getting married. In most instances, she knew the man for only a short period before taking the plunge.

My mom's final marriage was to a man named Jim. A 20 year Navy veteran and an all-around nice guy. I met Jim when they picked me up at the airport coming back from one of my jaunts to Tucker. Jim, being the gentleman that he was, carried my bags for me as my mom and I reconnected after a month's absence. What he didn't know was that I had carried weights to Georgia to work out with while I was there. In subsequent years, Jim never tired of telling the story about having to carry those suitcases with weights to the car, with his arms almost dragging to the ground.

I believe my mom married Jim as a marriage of convenience. She was tired of working, typically as a cashier or waitress, and she wanted an easier life for herself. Jim fit the bill as the hardest working man I've ever seen. He worked two jobs, and it wasn't uncommon for him to leave the house by seven a.m. and return about eleven p.m. He also worked long shifts on the weekend.

This gave my mom the easy life she hoped for, and for Jim, well, not so much. I once asked Jim if he thought my mom ever really loved him. In his own inimitable way, he said, "I've asked myself that question many times," a classy way of saying no.

In later life, my grandmother lived with us, and my mom treated both her and Jim like dirt. I am embarrassed to write that sentence because they were both two of the nicest, kindest, most peace-loving people you would ever meet. Unfortunately, that was exactly the kind of person that she would target to bully. The abuse she doled out was more psychological than physical but still quite painful to endure.

This is a side of my mom that is difficult to write about. I was never targeted by her with those tactics, but it was hard to see others endure such treatment. In classic bully fashion, my mom would always tell everyone that it was, in fact, she who had to endure the cruel bullying of others. I don't know if she really ever believed that or not, but she may have.

An example of how she treated Jim were the "dinner in a can" stories. You would think that with my mom being home all day and Jim working inhuman hours, there would be a nice, home-cooked meal waiting for him when he finally returned home. After all, isn't that the least she could do for such a man? Sadly, it was not the case. More often than not, Jim would return home to his "dinner," which would look something like this: on top of the stove would sit a pot, and in that pot there would be an unopened can of beans and a can opener. Ah, looks like fine dining again tonight.

Jim once told me that many times he thought, instead of coming home, he should just keep on going. No one would have blamed him, but Jim's downfall was that he was just too much of a good man to do that.

My mom never really had many friends. Oh sure, during the good times there were people who would come around for the food and the booze, but when those dried up they would disappear. An exception to this was her true friend, a woman named Sue.

Sue and my mom met when we rented a property to her and her husband. Sue remained a friend afterward for decades, becoming somewhat of a second mom to me. Notwithstanding my mom's brief marriages, most of the time it was just my mom and me. My much-older brother had been out of the house for a long time by then.

We would go over to Sue's house, often on Friday nights, and she would prepare us tacos and other treats, which I still remember fondly. Sue was a woman very much like Jim and my grandmother: sweet, nice, and peace loving. I'm glad my mom did not give her the same treatment that Jim and my grandmother got.

In her later years, Sue had many health problems, along with economic challenges. It is one of the great prides of my life that I was in a position to make her life a little easier. She ended up in a hospice-type facility, where I would visit her regularly. The last time I saw her, she told me she was getting very sleepy. We bid each other goodbye, as we typically did, but this time was different. She told me she loved me, and I told her the same. We both knew we were saying our final goodbyes on this earth, and she died shortly thereafter. Whatever mistakes my mom may have made in picking friends, Sue was a gold-medal winner. She was a true friend to my mom and to me.

Another family we were close to was the Harringtons. This was a family my mom met at church, and we stayed close to them throughout the years. They were a big family, with many sons and daughters. Dinner at their home was at six p.m. sharp every night. Everyone gathered around their huge, custom-made table and shared the events of the day. This was markedly different from my typical meals on TV trays in front of the television.

Through them, I was able to learn how large families operate, including the military precision with which the food was prepared. I am still close to that family, sharing Christmas Eve dinner with them, carrying on a 50 year tradition of us being together on holidays. I consider myself part of the family, and I believe they feel the same.

I wish I had more stories to share of my mom and the closeness we had, but this was not how it played out. She was older when she had me, and I don't feel she had the time or the energy to deal with raising a young son. That said, I will tell a few stories about our life together that may help to capture her spirit.

My mom always rooted for the underdog, and one of the few things we had in common was we both liked boxing. I typically knew more about the boxers than she did, and I would pick my "guy" prior to the fight, which would always include Joe Frazier if he was in the ring. As an aside, I got to meet Joe Frazier as an adult, and that was indeed a treat. I have a photo with him that I treasure.

Mom would watch the fight unfold, and invariably, with the ebb-and-flow of the match, there would be one fighter who was winning and another who was losing. Her allegiance would always go to the losing fighter, and she would begin rooting for him. Oftentimes, the fighter not doing well would rally and begin to pound the other boxer. My mom would then begin rooting for the other boxer, and so it would go throughout the match. Never before or since have I seen anyone change their rooting allegiance multiple times during a single fight, but that was my mother.

Another example of my mom's quirkiness was her purchase of a dining room set. The design of the set mimicked the look of large whiskey barrels. The backs of the chairs looked like such barrels, as did the pedestal for the table. The set was offered with the chairs in four different color choices: red, green, tan, and brown. The display at the store cleverly had one of each color set up so that customers could see exactly what their choice of color would look like on the actual chair. Customers would choose their color, presumably based upon their favorite color and the existing décor in their home. However, this was not how my mom rolled.

She told the store she wanted the set delivered with the chairs like they were in the display: one in each color. Thus, for many years we had a dining room set that had chairs of four different colors. Who does that? Only Trixie Jo. My guess is the salesmen talked about that one for a long time afterward.

Although I was raised by a single mom during a time when it wasn't as accepted as it is now, my mom did some really good things to help me grow as a boy. She arranged for me to have tennis lessons, a sport I have played throughout my life. She ensured I had swimming lessons, a critical life skill beyond simple recreation. She allowed me to participate in Little League, a great American tradition. I was involved in the Cub Scouts, and although I never moved into the higher ranks of scouting, that was a great experience for me, too. Perhaps most important, she always ensured we had a roof over our heads and food on the table.

Lest anyone think otherwise in reading this book, I loved my mom, and she certainly loved me. Life was difficult for us, with me growing up from a boy to a man, and we both struggled with that transition. She was a flawed individual, to be sure, as we all are, but ultimately there was much goodness in her.

I know she was proud of me, both as a boy and a man, and we made the journey together. We both did the best we could do, and my life has turned out extremely well. If she chooses to take a bow and claim some credit for it, who am I to argue? As they say, the proof is in the pudding, and I was able to create the life I wanted for myself, in part because she chose to give me life. I am grateful for that, and many other things. Thanks Mom…

7

YOU'RE JUST MEAN

Mom in her heyday.

My mom could be a very sweet person, but her strong suit was never in taking responsibility or accepting criticism. No matter what happened, it was never her fault. I'm sure you know people like this, but she took it even a step further. Not only was it not her fault, but there was a long list of people whose fault it was: crooked car salesmen who suckered her into a bad deal, shady real estate agents who "forced" her to sign a contract, people at work who had it in for her, and the crown jewel in her arsenal: people who were "just mean."

I fell into this last category on many occasions. Whenever I had her boxed into a corner with the facts on my side, instead of telling me I was right or that I had a point, I was told, "You're just mean."

Understand that my mom classifying you as "just mean," didn't make it so. It was simply a device for deflecting the blame onto you for whatever blunder may have occurred that traced directly back to her. This was the trump card when all other strategies failed, and it was, for her, the undisputed champion of them all. Rightly so perhaps, since once you were classified as mean, that was the end of the discussion.

In many ways, my mom was ahead of her time. She was born to play the victim, and she was a professional at it. It was almost as if she would purposely engineer things to go badly so that she could tell everyone that, once again, she had been "taken." One of her favorite sayings after being taken was, "Well, they saw me coming."

What she meant by this was that the bad people, the mean people, could smell an innocent victim like her a mile away. Once they saw her coming, it was only a matter of time until she got taken. This became so much of a family joke that whenever she would return from some sort of situation in which she could be taken advantage of, before she would even have a chance to speak, I would say, "Did they see you coming?" After giving me a look that I would describe as "How did he know?" she would go on to describe how she had been "taken to the cleaners," another of her favorite sayings.

I say she was ahead of her time because, in those days, no one wanted to be portrayed as a victim; that was the last thing you wished for. In fact, people would go far out of their way to persuade you they were not a victim even if it was clear they were. Not my mom; she wore it with the pride of an Olympic medal.

Nowadays, the culture in that regard has changed, and everybody wants to be the victim. I'm sure you've heard the arguments: "I'm the victim, here." "No, I'm the real victim." "No, I was the one who was victimized." How my mom got so far ahead of the curve on this one, I don't know, but she did.

A good example of her failure to accept any criticism or blame was in regard to her driving. She was a terrible driver, but like a lot of people, her perception was that she was a great driver, or as she would say, a very safe driver. Part of her reasoning for proclaiming herself a safe driver was that she drove very slowly. In fact, as I described earlier, she refused to drive on the freeway, classifying it as too dangerous. The fact that all the cars were going in the same direction, with no stop signs to run or traffic signals to blow, was not persuasive.

As I pointed out to her many times, you could be driving the speed limit and run people over in the crosswalk, something I'm very surprised she never did. Further, if you're going very slowly, and the overall traffic flow is going faster, then it is actually the slower speed that is unsafe. They say that speed kills, but my experience dictates this is a simpleton argument. It is actually disparity of speed that has more potential danger.

One of my favorite driving stories involved my brother's motorcycle. He had parked it on the street outside the house, when my mom arrived home and promptly ran it over as she was attempting to do what most people would call parking. Surely this would result in an outburst of self-blame. It was not to be. She came into the house and announced to my brother and me that she had run down his motorcycle. My brother was none too happy with this, but my mother quickly announced that it had happened because he had parked it "funny." No acceptance of responsibility, no apology, nothing.

She continued on into the next room, and that was that. This was exactly the kind of behavior that drove us all nuts. We burned to have her once, just once, admit responsibility, but this dream resulted in not much more than waiting and hoping.

When I was close to getting my driver's license, I had the sad misfortune of having to get my practice driving with my mom riding shotgun. Always one for the melodramatic, whenever I would get within about a football field of another car, she would start screaming, crying, and grabbing the dashboard, a technique we called the "hand brakes."

You must be thinking I'm exaggerating. How could someone be screaming and crying as you drove? Well, all I can say is that I was a witness, so I'm hoping you'll take me at my word. It was not a fun experience.

When I couldn't take it anymore and pulled over so she could return to the driver's seat, her calm returned because her perception of safety went back to normal. Of course, the perception of safety and actual safety are two different things. Off she drove, with horns blaring at her every block or so. Most of the time she either didn't hear the horns or ignored them, but occasionally she would announce that in the car behind us there must be some mean son of a bitch, which she often abbreviated to S.O.B.

My stepdad, Jim, who was a pretty quiet guy, was once asked by my mom what he thought of her driving. Never one for sugarcoating, he said, "Describe your driving? Okay, it's jackrabbit starts and jackass stops." I think Jim had it about right.

When criticized about her driving, my mom had long put forward a defense based on hard data. She would say that she had been driving a long time and had never been in an accident or had a ticket. We deconstructed this argument many times, to no avail. "In regard to an accident, maybe you have not been in an accident, but what about all the accidents you caused while you went on your merry way, oblivious to everything?"

No sale. "There's no proof of that."

"Isn't an accident in large part luck? Let's not confuse the good luck you've had with good driving."

Again, no sale. "Everybody has luck involved, but the bottom line is that many people have been in an accident, and I haven't."

"As for tickets, there are great drivers who have tickets and terrible drivers who don't. There are certain types of violations that lend themselves more to getting tickets, and those are not the type of violations you are committing. An officer can write a ticket for going too slow or weaving from lane-to-lane, but these are not high-profile violations like speeding." Nope, no dice. Having no tickets equated to a perfect driving record, which meant she was both a good driver and a safe driver. In her evaluation, the combination of no accidents and no tickets was ironclad, irrefutable proof of being a safe driver.

So, one day she finally got into an accident. No one was injured, but the car was crunched. I obtained the police report, which listed her clearly at fault. In some states, as the result of an accident, police officers can issue you a ticket for the violation that caused the accident. You guessed it, she got a ticket for running a red light on top of the accident.

Of course, she blamed her friend, who was a passenger, for "running her tongue" and distracting her. Now I would never wish for my mom to be in an accident or get a ticket, no matter how many times she mouthed off and drove us all crazy. However, it did happen, and that was the new reality for her.

After some time had passed, I initiated a conversation about the accident and the resulting ticket. Her initial response was as expected. It wasn't really her fault. She was distracted, the other driver could have avoided it, and the police officer was out to get her—all the usual suspects. I anticipated this line of reasoning and let it play out. I painstakingly built my case against her with logic, strong rationale, and evidence.

I stated that despite her biased conclusions, there were independent witnesses, not involved in the accident, who gave statements that she blatantly ran the red light. Claiming distraction did not mitigate her actions in the least. Nor did her argument that the other party could have avoided the accident. Even if this was true, it has no bearing, as the party who had the green light does not have the primary responsibility to avoid the person who goes through the red light. As for the police officer, he can only write the report based on the available evidence, and the overwhelming evidence was that she was at fault. She remained uncharacteristically silent.

Now, to move in for the kill, the coup-de-grace. For all these years she had based her claim of being a good and safe driver on the fact that she had never been in an accident or had a ticket. Using a form of verbal Jiu Jitsu, I would use the strength of her own arguments against her. Finally, she would be forced to admit error, to accept what we had all known all along, that she was not only not a good driver, she was a terrible driver.

I would be a hero in the family. They would carry me off on their shoulders for this upset victory. It was Buster Douglas knocking out Mike Tyson. It was the Washington Generals beating the Harlem Globetrotters, on their home court no less. Finally, the queen would be humbled.

Okay, careful now, not to get overconfident. This final move was a dangerous one; don't try this at home. I told my mom that for all these years, her claim of being a good driver was hinged on her "perfect" driving record of no accidents and no tickets. Her claim was that this was undeniable evidence of her driving ability. Now she had both an accident *and* a ticket. By her own standard, this was undeniable evidence that she was not a safe driver. If having no accidents and tickets meant she was a good driver, then an accident and a ticket could mean one thing, and one thing only, that she was not a good driver.

"You can't have it both ways. You are not a good driver, much less a safe driver, and this is an assessment based upon your very own set of standards, so just admit it."

I had done my job, and her silence gave rise to that notion. This must have been hard for her too. After all the years of putting her "perfect" driving record in our faces, it would be a bitter pill to swallow that she had been beaten at her own game, with logic that could be attacked only by impeaching her own long-expressed philosophy. I sat back and waited for the inevitable admission, one we had all waited so long to hear. She looked me in the eye for what seemed like a long time before she finally spoke.

"You're just mean."

8

POPPA GEORGE

One of the only fun outings
with just me and my dad.

My father George was born in the South in the 1930s. I don't know much about his younger life, simply because he didn't volunteer a lot and I didn't think to ask. I know he spent time in the Army, although he did manage to miss serving in World War II by a few years. My father was never one to give me much in the way of advice, but he did share one piece of guidance he learned from his time in the service.

He told me how while with a large group of fellow soldiers, one of the sergeants came in saying he needed a volunteer, but it had to be someone who could drive a jeep. My father imagined himself driving some general around, and that duty compared quite favorably in his mind to digging a ditch so he volunteered.

The sergeant brought him into the kitchen area and introduced him to the largest pile of potatoes he had ever seen. The direction given was not grammatically beautiful, but it was painfully clear: "Get to peeling!" After that episode, two things remained clear for my father. One, potatoes were never at the top of his desired food list, and two, he never volunteered again in his life.

He never went to college, but he discovered he was pretty good with numbers and began to get work with various firms in their accounting departments. He ultimately met and married my mother, but they had a rather stormy relationship, which involved a lot of drinking and fighting. My brother was part of the package when he married my mom, and my father ultimately adopted him when he was a young boy.

As my brother describes it, my father did not treat him very well, and I don't doubt this for a second. Many years later, my brother and I were having a conversation about George, and he told me he believed that he was never treated well because he was the son of another man, a war hero no less, who had died in battle in the Korean War. Of course, any real man would be honored to raise the son of such a person. Being a real man was perhaps not my father's greatest strength.

When I ultimately told my brother that I did not believe he got the poor treatment because of biological reasons, he seemed confused. I assured him that, although I was George's biological son, he didn't treat me that well, either. This was a burden my brother had always carried, and when I had convinced him that he wasn't the problem, it was George, a long-time weight lifted from him.

After living in the South, my mother and father got the idea, like a lot of other people, to move to sunny Southern California. They did just that, settling in the Los Angeles area. These were their glory days, I believe. George had steady work, and my grandmother was bankrolling much of the operation, so they lived pretty well. As I understand it, their house was party central for the "in crowd." They were blind to it at the time, but these were the type of fair-weather friends who were always there for you…as long as you kept the party going.

When my parents divorced, George met a woman named Pauline, who also hailed from the South. They made plans to start their lives together in Tucker in the mid-sixties. Years later, I chuckled when I read a memoir by the comedian Bob Newhart, who talked about his parents, George and Pauline.

Flying back to Tucker every summer to spend time with George and Pauline was always an odd experience. Except for the first time I went, when my father came to LA to fly back to Tucker with me, I always flew by myself as a little boy. Flying was quite glamourous then, unlike the tortuous grind it is now. People dressed up to fly and were usually pretty well behaved.

I always flew on Delta Airlines. They were headquartered in Atlanta, and my dad always said they had the best safety record. Of course, the real best safety record would have been if I had not had to get on a plane as a little boy to fly to see my father, who had moved all the way across the country.

During my flights, there was always one flight attendant who was assigned to check on me. I typically would read my books and mind my own business. I always made sure to ask for a deck of cards, which had the Delta logo printed on it. Anyone raised during those times as an only child was well-versed in how to play solitaire.

I remember hearing from someone that I could ask to see the cockpit; however, no one specified when this might occur, thus leading me to offer up a classic line to my assigned stewardess. About midway through our flight, when I was around 7 years old, I told her, "I'd like to see the cockpit now." She told me it might be best to wait until we landed. I have no doubt the ladies had quite a heehaw over that one: "Check out the balls on the kid in 28C. He wants to see the cockpit!"

Once arriving in Atlanta, I had my share of adventures, but the thing that has always struck me as strange is that there was literally zero time planned for father-son activities. Everything was either me doing things by myself or the three of us doing them. In all my years there, I can only remember one time where we did something that would qualify as father-son time, and that was not even a planned event.

On this day, I accompanied my father on his business rounds to see clients. Now, what could be more fun than that? It just so happened that coming home from the last call of the day, we went by a local attraction known as Stone Mountain. I believe my father just spontaneously decided to stop there, and it was probably the most fun I ever had with him.

We rode the train around the mountain, and it was particularly eventful because we got hijacked by Indians, who took over the train. Fortunately, the cowboys arrived and blasted the Indians, so we were able to continue on our way. I'm sure such activities would be outlawed today by the politically-correct police. We certainly can't have people engaging in stereotypes by enacting re-creations of how things actually were in the past. It is considered better now to pretend that cowboys and Indians did not act like cowboys and Indians.

We went on other rides while we were there. I still have, to this day, a picture of me taken by my father during this happy time. I was looking back toward him as the picture was taken during one of the rides. After that ride was over, we got chocolate ice cream cones, which were some of the best-tasting I've had. I think it was just because of the experience of the day. I believe my father had fun that day, too. I really don't know why we never did those kinds of things.

Pauline was an interesting woman. She was fairly tall and a bit stocky. Her burnt orange hair was usually well-coifed and piled high on her head, day or night. She never once left the house without being made-up and well-dressed. She had a fairly low-key personality and didn't seek drama.

Although she never said so to me, it was abundantly clear that her son, grandchildren, great grandchildren, and extended family were *way* above me on the food chain. I don't think Pauline really liked me, but I don't feel she disliked me, either. She just kind of tolerated me. Oddly enough, that is probably an accurate description of my father as well.

A good example of the smallness of Pauline related to letters I would send to my father. I addressed them, as you might imagine, to George Harvey. She told me that this was disrespectful, and I should address them to George and Pauline Harvey. I said there might be times where I wrote letters to both of them, but there might be times I wished to communicate solely with my father. Who knows, there might also be times I wished to communicate only with her as well. She still insisted that I should address letters to both of them.

Even as a young boy, I intuitively understood the concept of picking my battles, and I let this one go. Particularly so because I knew there was literally zero chance of my father siding with me over her on this issue, or any other issue.

I never called my father "Dad," or any other similar term of endearment. I think it was because I didn't feel he deserved that sort of title. I never called him anything. I would just start a sentence with whatever I wanted to say without any designation. There were times he and Pauline questioned me on this, but I never changed my practice. Rightly or wrongly, I guess I just didn't feel comfortable addressing him this way with his status as a one-month-out-of-the-year father.

Pauline had been married before and had a son named Ben Jr., who was somewhat of the classic fuck-up son. Despite his lack of accomplishment in life, his ego was firmly intact, and it was clear he thought the world of himself. One of my favorite stories about him involves my father's pontoon boat, which was one in a series of my father's never-ending impetuous and hare-brained schemes.

Within driving distance of my father's house was a recreational body of water known as Lake Lanier. My father decided he wanted to be able to go out on the water with friends and family, so he purchased the pontoon boat. This despite his never previously having expressed much interest in water-based activities. A pontoon boat is a large, rectangular boat, not built for speed. Rather, you get out on the lake and float around while you eat food and drink beer.

One day while we were out on the lake with Ben Jr. and family, my father decided that I should pilot the boat. It was not overly taxing, and there were no complaints about how I handled the duty. At the end of the day, we were steaming into the dock. As we got close, Ben Jr. pushed me aside, saying that I better let him drive the boat up to the dock. *Boom*! Ben Jr. lost control of the boat, and it smashed into the dock damaging the front end. I laughed so hard I could have fallen off the boat. That incident is Ben Jr. in a nutshell.

Another good pontoon boat story involved Mr. Spires, who worked for my dad around the property as a handyman. On one particular part of the lake, if you knew where to go, you could "beach" the boat and walk through the trees to get to a diner, which had a country-style gas station in front. If you were at the diner, you would certainly not be expecting anyone to just walk out from the forest area.

As we cleared the trees and moved toward the diner, there was Mr. Spires sitting in his pick-up truck at the gas station. The look of shock on his face was priceless. He clearly did not know that people would, on occasion, run their boats aground and go through the trees to the diner. Even had he known such a thing, he still would have been shocked to see that it was us that emerged.

My father worked very hard in the sixties and seventies. He made a lot of money, but he also spent a lot of money. He liked to have newer cars, and each year I arrived he would talk to me about whatever the newest car's capabilities were. Invariably, he would say, "This mother will flat out get it!" which was George-speak for a fast car. In addition to the pontoon boat, there were many other boondoggles that drained his money.

There was the Cessna-like airplane. In addition to the money to buy it, there was the money to maintain it, to store it, and the cost to take flying lessons since he had never flown before. Like the pontoon boat, and many other things that seemed like a good idea at the time, eventually these things were sold at a loss.

There was the investment in the alligator farm in South America. Shockingly, this one did not pay off. Who knew? Then there was the catalytic conversion plant in Utah that was going to be removing the platinum from old catalytic converters. The cash would roll in on this one—until it didn't.

Then there was the coin-operated car wash. Put in your money, drive on through, and in no time your car would be clean as a whistle. Best yet, it was all automated, so there were no workers and no payroll. We'll be turning those quarters into millions in no time. Amazingly though, that one didn't become profitable.

One of the most interesting ones was known as the Jolly Chef and was located in Alpharetta, Georgia. This was a small-town cafeteria. My father got the idea to buy this one based on his extensive experience in the restaurant business. Oh, wait, he had no experience in the restaurant business.

Not to fear though, Ben Jr. was somehow available to run the restaurant. Even better, it was an all-cash business, so there's no way that could fail with Ben Jr.'s high level of competence, trustworthiness, and extraordinary experience in the restaurant industry. Oh, wait on that one, too. For reasons that just can't be understood by mere humans, this venture went down the tubes as well. Something good did come out of it. I still have a wooden nickel with the Jolly Chef name printed on it. So you see, it wasn't a total loss.

I could go on and on, but I won't. You get the idea. My dad was wildly successful at his home-based accounting business, but unsuccessful at virtually everything else. It provided him a very good living, which could have translated into multi-millionaire status had he simply stuck to what he knew how to do and invested the revenue in conservative ways.

In the final analysis, my father was what is commonly called a "character." He viewed himself as a bit of a player with all of his "investments." He believed he was the kind of person other people liked to be around because you just never knew what he might say or do. "That George is a character!" My viewpoint is that his self-image was quite different from how others viewed him. I think they tolerated him more than embraced him, and this was particularly true of Pauline's family. Everyone fails in the accuracy of their self-assessment; it is just a question of degree, and George may have had a bit more disconnect in this regard than most.

I guess we all have to be who we are in the end. Though I was only on site for one month out of the year, with his business to attend to, along with managing whatever the debacle of the moment was, there just was not much time for him to be a father. Even the demand to be a father for only one month out of the year proved to be overly taxing for him.

That's okay, though. I learned a lot from my dad, albeit mostly what not to do, particularly as a father. Sometimes, those can be very powerful lessons, and I have taken them to heart in my role as a dad.

9

THE HOUSE AND THE LAWN

On the lawnmower in front of the creek,
with the crossing panels in view.

It was kind of a random thing that my father, George, and his wife, Pauline, settled in the small town of Tucker, Georgia. They both had strong roots in the southern portion of the United States, primarily in Mississippi. However, as they toured the South as a newly married couple, they somehow stumbled upon the town and found a home they thought suitable to their needs. This proved to be a good choice, because as far as I could tell, they were very happy both in the house and in Tucker. They lived in that same home for several decades.

Tucker is an unincorporated county area founded in 1892 as a railroad community. It has retained its small-town feel over the years, and even now the population is only about 35,000. Presumably, it was less than that during the sixties. I think they liked the feel of Tucker as a small town, but it was positioned within close striking distance of the large city of Atlanta. Amazingly, as I was finishing this book in 2016, the citizens of Tucker voted to incorporate and officially become a city.

In the show *Sex and the City,* there are four lead characters who live out their lives in New York. It's been said that New York was such an important element to the show, that it was almost a fifth lead character. I feel the same way about the house in Tucker, where I lived cumulatively about a year of my life, so I'll describe it to you in detail.

It was a brick home built in the early-sixties, set on over three acres. The home was surrounded on both sides by large driveways, one which led to the upper part of the house, and one which led to the lower basement portion. There was a big grassy area in front, but the real beauty of the property was in the back. A sloping grassy area with huge pine trees led down to a creek. Across the creek, the property continued on, before sloping upward toward the property line.

The main house had an attached carport, as was the typical custom in that area. There were three bedrooms and two baths, along with the living room, which was used entirely as my dad's home office. A kitchen, laundry room, and dining/sitting area completed the main floor. Below, there was a full basement, which was huge, but not yet "finished" when they bought the house.

Soon thereafter they completed the basement area with two bedrooms, two baths, and a living room and kitchen area. The idea was to rent out that portion of the property, which had its own entrance through the driveway that led down to that basement area. Although you could enter that living area from the outside, you could also enter through an interior staircase, which I found quite beneficial. All-in-all, it was a truly terrific property, and I give George and Pauline high praise for their choice.

There was a very nice man, named Jack, who rented the newly finished basement area. He had worked with my dad before my father had created his home-based business, so they were on very good terms. Jack worked during the daytime, which meant that I had, in essence, my own bachelor pad as a child. No one seemed to care that I spent time there while Jack was gone to work. Some of my escapades down there will be captured in later chapters, but for now, suffice to say it was a pretty good setup.

I was in Tucker during the summer months, and the weather was always very hot. As the old saying goes, it's not the heat, it's the humidity, and Tucker was one of the greatest representations of this I've ever known. It's hard to describe to someone who has not experienced it, but perhaps the most common description is that when you walk outside, it's like going into a sauna. It's sort of like breaking into an immediate sweat.

Choosing Tucker as a home base made a lot of sense for George and Pauline, but the summer weather was one thing that was not to their liking. They liked it cold inside the house, and I mean cold. I don't know for sure what temperature they kept the air conditioning at, but it would not surprise me in the least if it was somewhere in the low sixties. I don't ever remember the air conditioning unit kicking off. I didn't mind it, but moving from the house to outside was an almost unbelievable change. I have no idea what the electric bill was like, but they didn't care.

Central air conditioning was not a common thing in Tucker at the time, so it was truly a great luxury during those incredibly hot summer months. It was the oddest thing, though, that if you stood on the front lawn and looked at the living room windows, you could actually see condensation on the inside of the windows; that was how cold they kept it in the house. To me, the constant chill of the house became as much a part of the home as the décor or the wall color. I just can't imagine it being hot in that house.

One of the major challenges of such property was something as seemingly simple as mowing the grass. The mere size of the property made this quite a chore. There were times that my dad hired someone to do it, but during my years of summers in Tucker, this was one of the few jobs he took on himself. It would have been possible to cut all that grass with a standard mower but what you really needed was a riding mower. I first arrived in Tucker when I was about 6 years old, and I had never seen a riding lawnmower before. As you might imagine, a boy that age would be quite interested in such a machine.

During my month in Tucker, we might mow the grass a couple of times, but it was always an adventure. One of the things that made it somewhat of a high-wire act was that there didn't seem to be any way to mow the lawn without my father knocking back a number of beers. What kind of a fool would get on a riding lawnmower with a deadly sharp rotating blade without first having your thirst sufficiently quenched?

In the early days, we typically rode together on the lawnmower, with my father in "control" of it. As you can see by the quotation marks, I use the word control rather loosely. Further exacerbating the problem was the creek, which seemed to be quite a magnet for the lawnmower. The creek was also an endless source of fascination for a young boy.

There was one particular area of the backyard that had an especially steep incline. During one mowing session, we powered up the hill, only to have gravity intervene and cause us to backslide toward the creek. We made another run at it, this time with my father giving it more gas. Again, we backslid without gaining enough traction to crest the hill. The third time's the charm, right? We moved the mower all the way back to the creek, and my father began gunning the engine to get up as much power as we could before we hit the incline. He dropped it into gear, and away we went.

This time we made it to the very crest of the hill, and it looked for a moment as if we were going to make it. I can only think that he had done this many times before, but that with my additional weight, the equation had been thrown off. The front of the mower began to rise upward, only a little at first, but then higher and higher until the mower tipped over backward completely. This threw us from the seat of the mower, and we watched from the ground as the lawnmower cartwheeled end-over-end down the hill until it tumbled into the creek.

My dad and I stared at each other for what seemed like a very long time, both knowing we could have been killed or mutilated. He finally gathered himself and spoke. He simply said, "I think that's enough for today."

On the good news side, the lawnmower's engine had shut off. We went back to the house so that he could get another beer and properly process what had happened. We regrouped and managed to fish the mower out of the creek using ropes and a nearby tree. The mower was sent off to the repair shop. I was not privy to the conversation between George and the lawnmower shop owner, but I've often wondered what he told him about how the mower ended up in the condition it did.

Another mower challenge was getting across the creek, where there was a large area of grass that needed to be attended to. Initially there was a pair of wood planks bridging the creek, but at some point this was upgraded to a pair of iron rails, which would allow you to drive the lawnmower "safely" across the creek. I wasn't privy to what happened to motivate the upgrade from wood to iron, but my belief is it was not done by my father as a proactive safety measure. Although this was certainly a good enhancement, there were still some obstacles involved.

First, although the wheels of the mower would fit into the channels of the rails, there wasn't much margin for error. Second, there was a substantial downslope leading to the rails, meaning that as you lined up the wheels with the rails, gravity was pulling you downward at an uncomfortable rate, so you had a very limited amount of time in which to get it lined up properly. Third, without exception, my father was plastered when he would carry out this operation.

One of the very few times my dad used good judgement in regard to me was in the crossing of the creek. He would not allow me to be on the mower when he made the crossing. Instead, I had to get off the mower, wait for him to cross, walk across the rails myself, and then join him on the other side.

On more than one occasion, I watched him as he lined up the wheels with the rails in a way that did not seem to make sense. It was almost as if he saw the rails in a different place than they actually were or that he was seeing more than one set of rails and was guessing as to which set of rails were the actual ones. I would try and warn him when I saw this occurring, but with his tunnel vision and the loud engine going, there was not much I could do other than watch him drive the mower into the creek. Sometimes, he was able to jump off the mower so the machine would make the plunge solo, but other times he rode it all the way home.

As we gained experience, we became pretty good at getting the mower out of the creek. At no time was there any thought that perhaps we should handle the grass on the other side of the creek before having the first beer. That would have been inconceivable. Nor was there any consideration of replacing the two rails with one large platform, thus eliminating the challenge of lining up the wheels with the rails. Where would be the fun in that? I'm glad I had the lawnmower experiences, as I still chuckle about them to this day. I'm even gladder I wasn't killed or maimed during those adventures.

I will have fond memories of the Tucker house for the rest of my life. In fact, I dream about it on a fairly regular basis. To my knowledge, the house still stands today, and I hope to go back and visit it at least one more time in my life. It was a great place to grow up as a part-time Southern boy.

10

BUBBA

The LA house I grew up in,
with the infamous garage that ran afoul of Bubba.

At Sonny Bono's funeral, Cher gave a very moving eulogy. One of the things she said was that when she was young, the *Reader's Digest* magazine had a regular feature called, "The Most Unforgettable Character I've Ever Met." She said that, for her, that person was Sonny, and no matter how long she lived or how many people she met, that person would always be Sonny. For me, that person is my brother.

He was in high school when I was born, and as such, we did not grow up as brothers in the traditional sense. As a small child, my pronunciation of the word "brother" was not articulated in pristine fashion and came out sounding more like "Bubba." That was what I called him then, and now, more than fifty years later, I still call him that.

Technically speaking, he is my half-brother, but neither of us has ever looked at it in that way at all. Although we have the same mother and different fathers, he is my brother, period. His father was killed in battle in the Korean War. My brother was a small child when this occurred, and I am sure this shaped him in many ways, both known and unknown.

My mother ultimately remarried my father, George, who ended up adopting my brother. This, too, I'm sure had its effects, particularly so when I came along. He thought at the time that he was to be somewhat of a second-class citizen, and this was correct, but not for the reasons he may have thought. George just wasn't a very good father, whether the child in question was biological or adopted.

As I grew up, my brother and I were not that close, simply because of the 16 year age difference. Although he was not really in the father-figure category for me, he was somewhat of an adult authority as directed by our mother. This put both him and me into awkward positions, as we didn't have the typical relatively equal status that comes with being brothers. He was 21 years old by the time I started kindergarten.

My mother would call upon him to give me serious talks and administer discipline, which made the relationship at that time more parent-child than sibling-based. He even went so far as spanking me, something I thought wildly inappropriate then as well as now—not because of the spanking but because that level of authority was not a good position for a sibling to occupy.

In addition to the big age difference, my brother was a bit of a "wandering gypsy minstrel." He has it in his blood to be on the move and was often gone to parts unknown as I was growing up. Among other things, he was a professional musician and traveled accordingly. Occasionally he would show up for a few days unannounced.

I remember when I was about 14 years old, I woke up around one o'clock in the morning at the apartment I shared with my mother. The reason I woke up quickly became evident, as there was a man rifling through my closet. I evaluated my options to deal with this situation. I was quite a tennis player at the time, and I had several metal rackets that were leaned up against my nightstand. My plan was to jump out of bed as quickly as possible with the tennis racket in my hand and attack the intruder with everything I had. Even as a 14 year old, I was riding up pretty close to two-hundred pounds, so I intended to give a good showing of myself.

Shortly before I was to make my move, the intruder must have somehow sensed that I had awakened, because, without even turning around, he said, "Que paso?" (Spanish for, "What's happening?"). I realized that a real burglar would probably not say this, but more important, I recognized the distinctive sound of my brother's voice. Of course, Bubba had stored some of his clothes in my closet prior to his last excursion. And so it went with Bubba's periodic entrances and exits in my life.

One of my very favorite things about my brother was that he never treated me like a child, and he was the only one who did this. He spoke to me as you would an adult and seemed as interested in my viewpoint and perspective as he did other adults'. I've always been grateful for this because I never really felt like I was a child. I always felt like I was an adult who was just waiting for my body to catch up. Whether he identified or sensed this in particular about me, I don't know, but I loved how he treated me and wished everyone would have done the same.

I have some great memories of my brother and me in my early teens. During the summer, we would take off on late-night adventures, something all young boys wish to do. We would go and play tennis at midnight, or get a chili burger at the famous LA burger stand, Tommy's, which was then, and is still to this day, open 24 hours. Marathon gin rummy games would carry on into the wee hours. We would go to Hollywood to eat or see a movie. I remember one occasion where we went to see a triple feature of James Bond films: *Dr. No, From Russia with Love,* and *Goldfinger.* Looking back, these were some of the most fun times of my life.

Despite all this, my brother and I are as different as night and day in our makeup. There was a popular television show in the eighties called

Simon & Simon. It was about two brothers who were in business together as private detectives. The older brother was Rick, and he was a nonconformist who could slide a little bit to the shady side, and reliability was not always his strong suit. The younger brother was AJ, who was much more traditional in his behavior, conservative in nature, and inherently reliable. As the brothers worked the cases there were numerous clashes due to the varying personalities and approaches of each brother. For those familiar with the show, that was me and Bubba, with him playing Rick and me playing AJ.

Although I'm not sure I needed the show to validate this concept, I never went into business with my brother, as it would be like two people working together who were not on the same page, and sometimes not even in the same chapter. A weird coincidence about the show was that my brother's nickname for me was AJ, something I've rarely been called. The Simon brothers fought like cats and dogs, but their love for each other was indisputable. No matter the situation, they always closed ranks when facing any outside threat.

A friend of mine, who ghost writes a comic strip, has met and often heard about my brother from me. She wrote a comic that was inspired by him. It shows the lead character being interviewed for a job by a company manager. When asked about his employment history, the character replied he really didn't have one, it was more like "a series of funny stories." As such, I will round out this chapter with some stories about Bubba that will illustrate him in a way that I think would be more effective than merely continuing to describe him.

Bubba chased women as dogs chase cats. It was an utter sporting event for him, and he had a shamelessness and courage about it that was legendary. It was a bad outing when he didn't get at least one phone number. The odd thing was, there were many numbers he got that he never even called, something I've never done in my entire life. I'm sure some of the numbers he got may have been phony, but often he would not know, as he never called the number.

Now why would a man badger a woman for her number if he wasn't really that interested? The best analogy I can give you is one that involves baseball. Why do players take batting practice? The answer is, to better help them hit the ball when playing in an actual game. I think it was this way for my brother, perfecting his patter, approach, and technique required repetition in order to be on top of his game when he was pursuing a woman he actually was interested in.

Although this was not my cup of tea, I learned that women enjoyed being told what they wanted to hear, and this is probably true of men as well. I don't think there was ever a waitress we had in a restaurant who was not told she had, "the most beautiful eyes." Now, why can't I be smooth like that?

We were once eating in a restaurant where our table in front was next to a big picture window that looked out onto the sidewalk. I noticed an attractive girl walk by as I leaned my head down to eat another bite of my sandwich. When I looked up, my brother was no longer sitting in his chair.

As I turned my head to the right and then to the left to see what happened, I caught the image of him running down the sidewalk after that same girl. No, the police were not called. When he returned from his mid-meal jog, he didn't have a number, but sometimes you strike out even in batting practice. I didn't get that good of a look at this girl, but I have the strangest feeling that her eyes were quite beautiful.

Bubba and I once had an opportunity to attend a Halloween party at the *Playboy*® mansion, and for Bubba this was like taking a dog to a sausage factory. However, because the girls there each had a line of men three deep, he took a more strategic approach. One girl was there with her father, and instead of approaching her, he went right up to her father and raved about the man's colorful pocket handkerchief.

This was an older man, and although he was happy to receive the compliment, he could not for the life of him remember where he got the handkerchief that Bubba so admired. This conversation ultimately led to the father introducing my brother to his daughter! Genius or treachery? I'll let the reader decide that one, but I will say that every time throughout the evening we ran into the old guy, he was racking his brain trying to remember where he bought the hanky.

My brother's lifetime-friend, Tim, once shared with me a scene he had seen in the Steve McQueen movie *The Thomas Crown Affair.* The lead character showed up one morning and said to himself, "Who do I want to be today?" Tim said that summed up my brother, and I agree.

We were once cleaning out a closet and found what both my brother and I agreed was the ugliest tie we had ever seen. Bubba, who tends to laugh louder and longer than anyone else, was in hysterics about what kind of a person would wear a tie like that. We had no end of fun- making about that tie. About a year later I was going through some old pictures and I found one of someone wearing that exact same tie: yep, my brother. When I confronted him with the photo, it was the only time I can remember him responding to anything with dead silence.

As the wanderer that he was, my brother would often acquire things that he could not take with him on his travels. An example was a relatively new electric washer and dryer, which he decided to store in our family garage. About a year went by and he returned to reclaim his appliances, but they were gone.

When he asked my mother about his cherished items, she told him, "Huh, those things were obsolete. I got rid of them." In her world, an electric dryer was obsolete due to the high cost of operation. The fact that she got rid of them, gave him no fair warning prior to taking that action, and expressed utterly no remorse for getting rid of them, tells you much about my mother.

Of all the ways my brother and I are different, one of the most obvious is temperament. He is very placid, and I am a volcano that is never too far away from erupting. His reaction to my mom's statement was probably the angriest I've ever seen him. I think it was not that he had lost his appliances, it was the complete apathy in my mom's voice in delivering the news that set him off.

At one point, there was a movie being made next door to our house. The movie was called *Forever Young,* with Mel Gibson and Jamie Lee Curtis. As is commonplace in the industry, the movie company compensates close neighbors in order to ensure their cooperation with filming. At the time, my brother lived in an upstairs apartment on the property. We expected the company to approach my mom to construct a cooperation deal, and in fact, they came to the house in a timely fashion.

What was odd was that they told us they had the check ready. To me, this seemed pretty presumptuous that we could just be bought off with whatever amount they decided. Since we lived literally next door to the house where they would be doing all the filming, we could make life difficult for them with barking dogs, loud stereos, use of outdoor lighting, and other annoyances. The representative handed over the check to me and my mom, and we saw that it was for a very reasonable amount. However, we also noticed that the check was made out to my brother.

Naturally, he had already made his own deal on a house that was not his without telling us. This was, fortunately, corrected in short order. In the end, it was fun to see the movie, which showed my mom's house in the neighborhood on several occasions. The house was also seen a few times in the horror movie *Shocker.*

Although throughout my lifetime my brother has typically had a shortage of funds, this never stopped him from having an entitlement mentality. The only thing I can figure is that it was left over from a time in our family when we were much more affluent. Further, he seemed to think that others should pay his way.

I've always been very generous with him in this regard. Pretty much anytime we did anything, I would pay, and if I wasn't willing to pay in a given circumstance, then I would not agree to go. I remember a trip we took to Las Vegas where I paid for everything, including a separate room for him. He never once took out his money, except for twenty dollars to use on the slots.

We had lunch just before we left, which I paid for as well. When he saw the tip I left, he was critical that it was not enough for our waitress with the beautiful eyes. Now that takes nerve when someone comps you a trip to Las Vegas and you criticize the tip they leave. My brother was never short in the nerve department. He did get to experience the volcanic temper part of my personality for his trouble.

Then there is the story of the demolished three-car garage, a legend that has lived on in family lore. Our house at the time was a brick structure, and there was a separate three-car detached garage that was also made of brick. One of the garages even had a brick floor. The other two had cement flooring, leading us to believe that perhaps it started out as a one car garage and at a later point two more garages were added.

In any event, one day my brother decided these garages must be demolished, as the mortar in between the bricks was powdery. I'll never know what made him determine this at that exact moment in time, but once he decided, he was on a mission.

As a young man of about twelve years of age, I felt this initiative was ill-conceived for a variety of reasons. First, the house dated back to 1935 and the garages perhaps even further, and yet they were still standing as of this time in the seventies despite some very nasty earthquakes that had occurred. Second, two sides of the garages actually made up what was, in effect, a fence. If the garages were gone, our property would be wide open to adjoining properties. Third, shouldn't professional inspectors and ultimately a demolition crew be brought in if this needed to be addressed? Fourth, once the garages were gone, what was the plan for replacement, and how would this be funded? Lastly, if the garages truly were a hazard, might it not be better to just close them off and park on the property, which had more than ample space where many cars could be parked? After all, the garages were well-away from the main house, and even if they collapsed altogether, it would not impact the home itself. Unbelievably, my analytical skills were not solicited and the demolition began.

You might think that for a large demolition crew with bulldozers, this garage could be taken down in a few hours, and that probably would have been true had we had a large demolition crew with bulldozers, but we didn't. We had my brother and a long post.

Had I not seen it with my own eyes, I would not have believed it. Over a period of weeks, Bubba took down the entire three-car brick garage armed only with a post. He did this by smashing the post against the bricks and creating openings. Some of the time he could do this from outside the garage, but other times it could only be attacked from within. Like a coal miner without a canary, he plunged into the garage and threw the post repeatedly against the wall.

Every so often he would come running out of the garage as another portion collapsed, just ahead of a pile of brick and rubble. The old saying, "Don't confuse good luck with good tactics" comes to mind, which was one thing he had in common with George. Bubba didn't have good tactics, but he did have the good luck not to be killed in the process.

So why the motivation all of a sudden to exert almost superhuman effort to undertake this task? Was it because of pleas from our mother? No, she did not want it done and was petrified as the process played out. Was it that he saw his duty and he'd done it? No, he had no such duty and was not similarly inclined to take on more mundane household chores like mowing the lawn. Was it that he was so inherently altruistic that he was simply acting in line with his incredibly charitable nature? Nope, strike three. I cannot say the reason with absolute certainty. I will simply comment that then, as now, used brick was worth a lot of money.

To conclude, I will remark that in an HBO special on the late actor James Gandolfini, one of his fellow actors said about him, "Jimmy was the opposite of bullshit." That is something I would hope that people would, either now or at least one day, say about me. I would wager a lot that no one has ever said that about Bubba.

A woman named Mary McCarthy was once on the old *Dick Cavett Show* speaking about a lady who was a notorious prevaricator. She said that every word out of this woman's mouth was a lie, including "*and*" and "*the.*" Perhaps that's a little bit of an extreme description for my brother, but there are times he has played in that arena. That said, I love him with all my heart and I always will.

11

DRIVING THE CAR

I took my driving seriously, even then.

In the sixties, everyone drove cars just as we do now. However, there were many differences as compared to today. My mom and dad both owned Cadillacs through the years. This was true in both good financial times and bad. Whatever other sacrifices needed to be made, you always wanted to be behind the wheel of a Cadillac. My father took it to an extreme by getting a new Cadillac every few years. I even remember one of the license plates: RUN 300.

This was quite appropriate, as my father George liked to drive fast, one of the few traits I think I inherited from him. If the conditions allowed and I could get away with it, I would drive one-hundred fifty mph everywhere I traveled.

Although I'm sure my dad enjoyed getting to his destination quickly, I don't think that was really the primary motivating force. He was always an anti-government guy; he absolutely hated the government controlling his life in any way. In fact, I never heard him refer to the "government." Instead, it was always "the damned government." I believe driving as fast as he wanted was simply another way to extend his middle finger at government control. Now that I think about it, I may have inherited that characteristic as well.

My father had a very tenuous relationship with the Georgia State troopers. It was kind of like the cobra and the mongoose. They were just born enemies. It was a constant test of skills and wills as each tried to outsmart the other. As technology developed, the troopers employed radar on the highways to catch speeders. My father countered with the "Fuzzbuster."

This was the earliest available device for detecting radar, and George always had it strapped to his sun visor. It was a bit sketchy in its performance. They got better over the years, but my father was never without one. One of the few times my dad would slow down was when it squawked.

A funny story emerged from this kind of driving when George was at the wheel and my brother was in the passenger seat. They were traveling on a Georgia highway when they came up on a fire truck with full lights and siren going. Now most people would stay behind the firetruck and give it a wide berth, as it was traveling at seventy-five mph, the existing speed limit at the time. Again, my father was not most people. He passed that firetruck like it was standing still with no hesitation about it. My grandmother would have said he passed it "like a freight train passing a tramp."

This gave rise to him saying many times after this, "Remember that firetruck we passed?" This is not a statement you get to make every day and he relished every bit of it. It is a funny statement on its face because of the seeming absurdity of it, but it has always given us a laugh when we bring it up. Moreover, it has stood the test of time, as I am now writing about it some 40 years later.

Seat belts were another bane of his existence. Although seat belts were installed in cars during those times, nobody actually used them. I can honestly say in all my time growing up, I never once saw anyone put one on. I know that sounds strange today, but that's just how it was back then. There were a lot of foolish things from those times, but failing to wear our seatbelts was a big one.

Eventually the car companies, prodded by the government I'm sure, began making loud buzzers on the car go off if the driver wasn't wearing his seatbelt. My dad took great pride in snapping the belt together while he was not in the seat and then stuffing it between the seat cushion and seatback of the car. This would "fool" the car into thinking he had his belt in place. That will show those bastards.

Another incredibly foolish thing done during those times was smoking. Everyone smoked. It was just the thing to do. My father even smoked a pipe. The house was bad enough with him smoking a pipe and his wife smoking cigarettes, but when we went on a road trip it was a nightmare. Imagine me as a young boy in the back seat, with both a pipe and a cigarette going perpetually up front. I'm surprised I didn't end up in an iron lung. Even young mothers-to-be smoked without a second thought. I don't wish to be too harsh in my criticism of these people though; they were just acting as people of their own time, just as we do today.

This reflected a very different time in parenting from now. In those days, the parents did whatever they wanted and children were told to keep quiet. The constant coddling that occurs nowadays with parents addressing the needs of their children every minute of every day were simply not in the cards in those days. Had I raised the issue of smoking in the car, I would have literally been laughed at.

Whenever I see older Hollywood movies, the actors are often smoking on screen as they did in real life. Smoking was part of their image both on screen and off, whether it was the "tough guy" or the sophisticated man-about-town. These images no doubt influenced many from that time to begin or continue smoking. The irony is that smoking ultimately killed just about every one of those actors. Arguably even worse was that it made breathing extremely difficult in later life, something of a form of torture in that you must struggle for every breath.

Pauline already had a nagging cough, which would erupt 4-5 times an hour. As she coughed and hacked for breath, my father would loudly chastise her by saying, "uh, uh" over and over again. Occasionally she would choke out something like, "I can't help it," but it would sound more like, "Ah caint hep it." Isn't it wonderful to have the comfort of a loving spouse? The radical idea of quitting smoking to mitigate a cough was never discussed.

The United States Surgeon General came out with the famous warning about smoking in 1964. Surely after that point no one could claim that smoking was not harmful, but what about before? My mother always said that by then she was hooked and couldn't do anything about it.

However, it seemed to me that even before the Surgeon General's report, common sense would dictate that it could not be a beneficial habit. After all, you are taking a plant, lighting it on fire, and inhaling the resultant smoke deep into your lungs, then rinse and repeat. How could that possibly not be bad for you? If you ran into a burning building would you take as many deep breaths of smoke as you could before you ran back out? No, you would avoid breathing to the extent possible. How is it that smoking would be any different?

The cigarette companies, accompanied by Hollywood, succeeded in making smoking glamourous during those times. So much so that the above-described common sense never really dictated people's choice to smoke. It became more of a choice of smoking or being considered a pariah, a social outcast.

As things tend to do, the opposite has become true now. Smoking is outlawed in almost all public venues. It seems funny now to think back to when you were greeted by a hostess in a restaurant with the question, "smoking or non-smoking?" In certain parts of the country this may still be going on. This was the interim step between allowing smoking everywhere and outlawing it everywhere, as is the current direction.

There is a scene in the great movie *Days of Wine and Roses* in which Jack Lemmon plays a young businessman who has become an alcoholic. Jack Klugman plays his Alcoholics Anonymous sponsor, who has come to visit him in his jail cell. The first thing he does is give him a cigarette. He then goes on to try and convince him that if he doesn't stop drinking, it will kill him. You got that? He is trying to keep him from killing himself with alcohol, but first gives him a cigarette! Talk about going out of the frying pan and into the fire. In real life, a sad irony was that both men died of cancer, no doubt from their real-life smoking habit.

Another of my favorite stories about cars and driving comes from a trip we made to our favorite restaurant, The Colonnade, an Atlanta institution since 1927. We ate out for dinner quite regularly at this fantastic place. This was our primary restaurant of choice, and it's still in operation to this day. If I return to Atlanta at some point, a trip to The Colonnade will be a top priority.

On one particular occasion we went with another couple, so there were five of us in the black Cadillac. My father never locked the car doors when he parked, and my guess is that during that time in that area it was a pretty common practice to leave cars unlocked. Even worse, he would not take the car keys with him. Rather, he would simply drop them on the floorboard of the car and when he returned to the vehicle, he would pick them up and start the car. I never knew why he did this, but I guess one advantage was that he would never have to worry about losing his keys.

However, on the night in question, we came back to the car after finishing our dinner and he could not for the life of him find the keys. As we all sat in the car, he fished around endlessly on the floorboard with no luck. We must have sat in the car for ten minutes trying to figure out what we were going to do.

At some point we noticed there were some things missing from the car. For example, we always kept a portable drink container on the floor in front. This was where Pauline would keep her endless supply of Tab or Diet Rite Cola, the ultimate form of diet soft drink "rotgut" at the time. We were perplexed in that if someone were to take the container and the keys, why not just take the car itself? As you may have figured out by now, we were in the wrong car. There was another black Cadillac parked next to us, and without even looking, we all knew we would find Pauline's Diet Rite Cola in that car. That's exactly what happened.

I've often thought about what would have happened had the driver of the other black Cadillac simply dropped his keys on the floorboard as my dad did. It's quite possible we may not have discovered we had taken the wrong car until we examined it more closely in the light of day the following morning. Yes, I know the story would be even funnier if that had happened, but I want to keep things as true-to-life as I possibly can.

One of my favorite memories is of the time my father just could not get past a VW Bug on the roadway. No matter what he did, that Bug always managed to stay in front of us. He reached a point where he just couldn't take it anymore, and he cut aggressively into a shopping center driveway as the Bug continued on. He took the backway behind the shopping center, which emptied out on the other side of the buildings. Coming to the end of the building you had to slow up quite a bit, as it was possible there would be another car coming that you could not see until you edged past the buildings.

As he moved forward, he was cut off by, you guessed it, the same VW Bug. In disbelief, all he could say was, "Well, I'll be damned." In his flustered state, though, it came out more like, "Well ah be damn," heavy emphasis on the damn. This set off furious laughter from me in the backseat, and I still smile about it to this day.

My dad was known to occasionally disappear for periods of time to drink and do who knows what. I believe this would properly be called going on a "bender." I don't know how often this happened, but I remember a couple of these specifically. Considering I was only there for one month out of the year, my guess is it was a semi-regular event. I remember one particular evening when he did not show up as planned and Pauline decided to go looking for him with me riding shotgun. I didn't know how she would know where to look, but there was one place we went that I'll always remember—the county jail.

She drove over to the jail and then specifically to a vehicle impound lot that was adjacent to the jail surrounded by a chain-link fence. We slowly drove by looking for his car. Even then, I remember thinking it odd she would be looking for him there, but she knew exactly where this lot was and thought it as logical as not that we might find him there.

Another time, while George was still living in California, we were with a woman he was dating at the time and we got pulled over by the police. I was very young then, and I saw my father get out of the car to go back and "confer" with the police officer. His reputation must have proceeded him, because even as a young child I told the woman, "They probably stopped him because he's drunk." I remember her telling me in a nice way, "Oh, don't say that." Out of the mouths of babes.

After my father moved to Georgia, he would on rare occasion just show up in California. I specifically remember we went to an amusement park, and he said he had to make a phone call. In those days you used a pay phone, and I stood by while he made his "person to person, collect call" to Pauline. He told her he was in California, and it was evident to me that this was going to be her first notification of where he was.

It seemed to me my father took a bit of glee in telling her this, thus enhancing his self-image as a really unpredictable type of guy. I don't know for sure, but my guess is that Pauline was prowling the county jail impound lot the night before.

My last car story involves the time my father drove in a parade—uninvited. He and Pauline were traveling through a small city on a Sunday and it just so happened they were having a parade, which made it difficult to navigate through the town. At one point, in his efforts to get through, he ended up turning left into the ongoing parade, fortunately in the same direction as the parade was heading.

Instead of pulling out of the parade at the first opportunity, he rolled down the windows of the Cadillac and waved feverishly to the crowd. Of course, they had no idea who was in the Cadillac, but he must be important, so they waved back. So, it went through the entire parade route, a certified public accountant who had finally found his fifteen minutes of fame in that RUN 300 Caddy.

12

NEE NAW

The Bat, with Rocky in the foreground.

I was a bit sickly as a child. I attribute this, at least partly, to my mother drinking, smoking, and doing who knows what else during her pregnancy with me. In those days, parents simply did what they wanted to do. In later years, my mom claimed she didn't know the consequences of her actions during those years, but that's difficult for me to accept because it seems to defy common sense.

Considering the effect liquor has on a full-grown adult, what could be the probable impact on a developing baby in the womb? How could ingesting smoke into one's lungs and bloodstream constantly throughout the day possibly be good for tiny, developing lungs? How could the constant haze of secondhand smoke in the house possibly be good for an infant trying to breathe? I don't think you need the surgeon general's advice on any of these things.

My belief is that even if such medical information was widely available at the time, they would have still done whatever they wanted to do because they could. Parents were much more self-centered in those days, whereas now we have the opposite, with children being self-centered and having their every comfort catered to by parents.

I developed jaundice, asthma, and a number of other ailments throughout childhood. The body has remarkable recuperative powers to heal itself, and ultimately I grew into a powerful athlete, successfully competing in sports like football, baseball, basketball, arm wrestling, shot putting, and tennis over many years, and even bench pressing 435-pounds in competition…at the age of fifty. In the beginning, though, I had some health challenges.

During one of my overnight hospital stays to evaluate my condition when I was very young, I was kept in a crib-like enclosure. As with the caged bird singing, the only way I could project my presence beyond that crib was vocally, and so I did, yelling "Nee Naw" incessantly at the top of my lungs. You'll note I wasn't yelling "Maw Maw," "Da Da," or "Bubba." It was Nee Naw because that was what I called my grandmother.

When my parents came in the next morning, the hospital staff I'm sure wanted to ask them, "Who the hell is Nee Naw?" but they more politely asked, "Who's Nee Naw?" My parents explained that I was calling for my maternal grandmother, Adeline.

Thus began a pattern in my life of looking to my grandmother for comfort, something that would last throughout my childhood and into adult life. It is interesting that even as a baby my instincts led me to call for her instead of my mother, father, or much-older brother.

In later childhood years, "Nee Naw" became "Nan," and in adult years, "The Bat," a name that must be explained. "Bat" is short for battleax, a nickname men often gave to their mother-in-laws back in the day. It was not a compliment. In Nan's case, I called her The Bat in the same way one might call a very large man "Tiny." It was an opposite-type nickname. At first my family members didn't like it, but it wasn't long before they were coming home and inquiring, "Where's The Bat?"

My grandmother was born in the Deep South shortly after the turn of the century, into what she would call "squally times." This was her term for periods where people were destitute, and she lived through many such instances in her lifetime. The arc of my grandmother's life is astonishing. When she was born, there was no such thing as a plane in the sky. In her lifetime, though, you could get on a plane and fly anywhere in the world and astronauts could fly to the moon and back.

She was a young girl during World War I, lived through the Great Depression and Prohibition and was a mature adult during World War II. She lived through the development of the nuclear age, the Korean War, the Vietnam War, and the Cold War. These are the kinds of experiences that shape a person, much different than today, where we navel gaze and obsess over the most trivial of things. People of her time were faced with survival, and thus had no time or energy for the types of things we are consumed with today.

She referred to her parents as "Mama White and Papa White." Mama White would mind the house and the children, and Papa White would take any work he could get. They were dirt poor, and Papa White would go out hunting in the woods every chance he got. Whether they ate that night or not would often be determined by whether he was able to kill an animal. I never knew Mama or Papa White, but I still have a glass flour container that belonged to Mama White. It is the only tangible link I have back to those times.

An example of their economic situation came at Christmas time. Getting actual presents was literally unthinkable. However, if it was a good year, she and her siblings would each get an orange, a very special treat indeed. In a bad year, of which there were many, you'd get nothing.

Many years later, when my wife and I first got together, I noticed that she had put an orange in each of our stockings at Christmas time. I knew

I had never told her this story and I asked her, "Why the oranges?" She replied that it was symbolic of Christmas to her, of the gratefulness we should have for our bounty of treasures in life, and that we should never forget how lucky we are. I was literally stunned at this gesture, and I then told her the story about my grandmother. She said that although she always believed in the concept of the orange, that was the first time she had actually placed oranges into stockings.

Nan grew up in the early part of the century and reached adulthood as the country moved into the "Roaring Twenties." In the late-twenties the depression hit and times got tough even for wealthy people. You can imagine what it was like for people who already had nothing. Somehow my grandmother survived and was in her late-thirties by the time of World War II. She had married and had my mom and my uncle Robert.

Her first marriage did not work out, but her second one, to a man named Will, did last. He was an older man and by all accounts a solid individual. He was a contractor and was somewhat well-to-do for the time. When he died, he left my grandmother fairly well off for the first time in her life. My grandmother never married again.

As a child, I consider myself to have been raised by my mother and grandmother, notwithstanding the yearly trips to Tucker. They were on the opposite ends of the spectrum in terms of personality. My mother was impulsive, tempestuous, and loved to create drama. Nan was quiet, reserved, and prioritized peace above all else.

During most of my childhood years, my grandmother lived in a large apartment building which she managed, thus gaining free rent for herself and a small salary. This, coupled with her Social Security pension and modest lifestyle, allowed her to live comfortably. Unfortunately, all of her previous wealth had been drained dry by my mother.

Nan enjoyed her peace and solitude but always kept her radio playing in the background. She loved to keep up on news and events and was typically the first one in the family to know of important things that had occurred. I still remember her calling me when Elvis Presley died.

My mother had a love-hate relationship with my grandmother, and it's a bit of a mystery as to why. Nan was the most easy-to-get-along-with person you will ever meet. Somehow my mother was able to take that and make it into conflict.

There were numerous times throughout the years that Nan would move in with us, always at the demand of my mother. Within a short time, my mom would kick her out. This cycle repeated itself many times throughout the years and was as mystifying to me then as it is now. How could anybody kick Nan out? In our family, it would be kind of like kicking out Mother Teresa. Further, if you couldn't get along with her, whatever your reasons, why in the world would you repetitively insist that she move back in? The only conclusion I can come to is that it was some sort of sadistic game my mother enjoyed playing.

You probably could not find more different people than me, my brother, my father, and my stepdad, Jim. However, one thing we all agreed on unequivocally was that my grandmother was one of the sweetest and best people we've ever known. Somehow my mother did not see it that way, although she had no hesitation whatsoever in using her whenever it suited her need.

An example of Nan's placement of my comfort above her own is her conversations with "Miss Roser." You see, when I was a very small boy and had to go "big potty," I wanted Nan to come in the bathroom with me and talk to Miss Roser. As I sat on the throne, she would sit on the ledge of the shower and pretend to be talking on the phone with Miss Roser. They would talk about the events of the day as I completed my business.

I don't know if Miss Roser was an actual person my grandmother knew or if it was a made-up name. I'm not sure why it was such a comfort to me for her to talk to Miss Roser during my time in the bathroom, but it was. I tell this story because it is a good example of how much she loved me. My guess is that talking to Miss Roser wasn't her idea of being a participant in the old *Queen for a Day* show, but she did it without complaint and that's an example of real love.

My times with my grandmother were some of my fondest moments on earth. I loved being with her and staying over at her apartment because there was simply love and peace there. In my house, with my mother, things were always near the edge, even when it was seemingly going well. This caused an anxiety that permeated the home at all times because you knew you were always only a minute away from a change in the direction of the wind.

Times with Nan were an example of the beauty of simplicity and simple pleasures. Cooking in her tiny kitchen, walking to the store, having a bite to eat at the local hole-in-the-wall, these were all things that gave me great pleasure and comfort. Her second story apartment looked out onto a very busy thoroughfare, and we both used to delight in going to the window to see the police cars, fire trucks, and ambulances go by with their lights and sirens. We could push out the screen and see them for miles away.

Below her apartment was a movie theater, which was managed by a friend of hers named Mr. Bang. Back in those days, believe it or not, the manager of the theater would typically sit out at his desk in the lobby. When we would go in, Mr. Bang would never charge us admission, so we got to see a lot of movies together. Sometimes there would be movies of the day, but often there would be classic movies playing like *Gone with the Wind,* and *The Wizard of Oz.*

It was a real treat to see those movies in color on the big screen, versus on the fifteen-inch black and white TV we had at the time. I remember seeing many Disney movies there like *The Love Bug, The Shaggy Dog,* and *The Computer Wore Tennis Shoes.* I can only remember watching maybe four movies ever with my mother, but I sure saw a lot of them with my grandmother.

One of my favorite incidents from these times was when they were showing a *Planet of the Apes* marathon, which included the original movie and the sequels. Although it was usually just me and Nan, on this one I brought along a friend. At one point in the movie, the "good" apes had evidently been killed on the battlefield by the "bad" apes and we were saddened by this.

However, just when you least expected it, the good apes, who were merely playing possum, jumped up and attacked the other apes, defeating them in short order. My friend was so into the movie that when this happened, he literally stood up, pointed at the screen, and shouted at the top of his lungs, "They were only faking it!" Even with the recent advance of 3-D technology, never before or since have I seen someone so engrossed in the motion picture experience.

Nan and I enjoyed watching TV as well. Our two favorites were wrestling and the roller derby, both of which were filmed at the Olympic

Auditorium in downtown Los Angeles. Children and older people have a great deal in common, and my grandmother and I completely immersed ourselves in the experience of those two events, falling hook, line, and sinker for all the pageantry and good versus evil storylines.

In wrestling, our favorite wrestler was the "Golden Greek," John Tolos, also known as "Maniac" Tolos in his later career. It should tell you an awful lot about me and The Bat that our favorite wrestler was known by this name. We watched religiously and enjoyed it to no end. During my time in Tucker every year, my grandmother would even write me letters with blow-by-blow accounts of what went on.

As I write this, I have a photo of John Tolos on my desk and an autographed photo in another room. It takes me back to a very special time in my life. A footnote: when John Tolos died, I actually went to the public service as a way of connecting with a time in my life gone by.

As for the roller derby, we loved it. We rooted for the LA Thunderbirds with skaters like Ralphie Valladares, Danny Reilly, and Shirley Hardman. We even went in person a couple of times. You haven't lived until you've seen a bunch of old ladies screaming for blood, and yes, my normally placid grandmother was one of them. She had a favorite term for those on the opposing team that she didn't like: "dirty dog." I remember one character in particular, named Dave Pound, who got the "dirty dog" pronouncement every single time he appeared on TV.

Tragically, Shirley Hardman drowned in her backyard pool in 1973. My grandmother was absolutely convinced that foul play was involved and someone from one of the opposing teams had murdered her. Much to her dismay, the FBI was never called in to investigate this situation.

Like a lot of people raised in the "country," Nan had many sayings she liked to repeat. Some of my favorites are listed below:

He hasn't got two pennies to rub together (said in regard to a particularly poor person).

They should put him up under the jail (said when a particularly nasty individual was so bad that placement in a standard jail cell simply would not be adequate).

I don't want to, but I will (said when carrying out a task that was not something she really wanted to do).

He's lower down than cat mess, and that's right on the ground (said about a particularly vile person).

You don't know what you have until it's gone (said to remind people to try and be more grateful).

He wouldn't pay a dime to see Jesus (said about someone who is very cheap).

You'll ruin a hand (said when someone, usually me, was engaging in some sort of activity that she perceived could cause injury to one's hand).

Nan never drove a car in her life, but this did not stop her from getting where she wanted to go. She was a big-time walker before it ever became popular as a leisure activity. She was always in motion, and walking was a big part of her life. It was always done as a means to an end, to get to a particular destination. I can't ever remember my grandmother going for a walk for fun or exercise; it was always with a purpose. She spent many years waitressing when she was younger, and that may have had something to do with it as well.

When walking was not viable, she would ride the bus, and she was fearless about taking the bus anywhere. One of my favorite childhood memories was of going to downtown Los Angeles with her in the sixties. In this era, the big stores were almost tourist attractions in and of themselves. There were big picture windows in front of the stores, and there were literally live shows that would be conducted in those windows. People would gather on the street to watch, and of course, the store hoped this would lead to them coming in and shopping. Clearly a time gone by, but one I remember fondly.

Before I could read, my grandmother would read to me. Oddly enough, although I'm sure she must have, I can never recall my mother ever reading to me. One particular book I never got tired of was about a critter named "Mushmouse," who was featured in a story with a cat he continually outsmarted. Nan read that one to me so many times I could take the book and simulate that I was reading it.

I had memorized the exact language on each page. As such, I could "read" the words on the page out loud, turning the pages at the exact right time. This made it possible that sometimes she would read the story to me and other times I would "read" it to her. I'm sure she must have gotten sick of that book, but you would have never known it. A few years ago I was able to track down and acquire that book via the Internet, and it is now a treasured possession that takes me back to a special time.

There is a beautiful song by the great singer-songwriter Bill Withers called, *Grandma's Hands.* It describes the beauty of the special relationship that often develops between grandmothers and their grandchildren, a relationship that can be quite different than that between those same children and their mothers. The song ends with the singer saying that if he gets to heaven, he'll look for Grandma's Hands.

Of all the memories I have of my childhood, the sweetest are of those with me and Nee Naw. She was always there for me, whether it was to cook for me, play ball with me, warn me of life's dangers, or convince me that I had what it took to be successful. I didn't have the best childhood with my mother and father, but I'll put my time with Nan up there with the best childhood times anyone could have. When I think of the blessings of my life, she is right there at the top of the list.

13

WALKING TO WORK

With Buzz Aldrin, the man in the moon.

Chuka-chuka-chuka-chuka-choo-choo-choo. Chuka-chuka-chuka-chuka-choo-choo-choo. Chuka-chuka-chuka-chuka-choo-choo-choo. Chuka-chuka-chuka-chuka-choo-choo-choo-choo-choo-choo-choo-choo.

This was the noise I woke up to almost every morning in Tucker. It was the sound of my father's manual adding machine. This large device had numbers you would push. Once you pushed them down to where they would hold, it made the "chuka" sound. When you hit the "total" button, the "choo" sound would occur. At the final end of your tabulations, you would hold down the total button and it would go into a long series of "choos." The sound that adding machine made is a noise that will stay with me the rest of my life.

I've heard it said about certain people that they were "ahead of their time." This is meant as a compliment, as any person can be of their time. To be ahead of one's time requires some sort of forward-thinking that allows a person to be involved in innovative things before they become common practice. In a general sense, I would not describe my father as being ahead of his time, but there was one area where perhaps this may have been the case. It involved him creating a business and running it from his home.

That might not appear like much these days, as it would seem that every other house on the block is running some kind of operation out of their home. However, back in the sixties this was not the case at all, thus resulting in my dad being ahead of his time.

I still have one of his business cards from those days: Harvey Bookkeeping Service: Efficient Service, Courteous, Reasonable Fees. The motto of the business was as follows: "We Specialize in Small & Large Accounts." Now even as a child that struck me as odd. How could you specialize in *both* small and large accounts? Wouldn't it be one or the other? If a prospective client called and stated he had a medium-sized account, would he be turned away? These questions proved trivial as the business was quite successful, affording my father a very comfortable lifestyle throughout most of his life.

The entire living room was the home office. There were three large work desks, allowing my father to have a place for seasonal employees to work alongside his desk. There were large filing cabinets and a huge set of shelves where accounts were kept in large binders enclosed in plastic-zippered containers.

The file cabinets contained files on just about everything you can imagine. As an accountant, files were a large part of my father's life. He had a file with all the letters I had ever sent him. He had a file for jokes he had come across. Perhaps the most amusing file was one titled the "Pauline Don't See File." And yes, this was the actual title on the file. In this file, as you might imagine, were things he wished to keep from his wife. Although he showed me this file, my suspicions were always that there was another file kept in a more discreet place that may have been labeled the "Pauline REALLY Don't See File," but I was not privy to this.

George was very much an early adopter of technology. He had one of the first home copier machines by Xerox, which led to people of my age for the longest time saying, "I need to Xerox this," instead of saying I need to copy it. Computers had not made their way into homes yet, but he did use computers in his work. This was done by taking various data to a commercial property where they maintained very large computers. We did this once a week or so and referred to it as the "computer runs."

He also had one of the first home answering machines, which may not sound like much now, but was quite a big deal at the time. The device was the size of two shoeboxes placed together long-ways, with a cord that would connect it to a typical phone. We had just gotten push-button phones, which replaced the rotary dials that required putting your finger in the hole of the digit you wanted and circling the dial around seven times until you had called the number you wanted.

In those days, you would get a "busy" signal when you called someone who was using their phone. This still occurs, but is rare. You would have to keep calling until the number would actually ring. There was no way to know how long the number would be busy. In rare emergency-type cases, you could call the operator and have her (yes, it was *always* a "her" back in those days) "break in" to the line. This was reserved for only the most desperate situations.

Oftentimes, the phone would ring many times, and no one would pick up. You would just have to keep calling back until someone answered. This is why in old movies you would often see a person open the door to the house with groceries in their arms and they would drop the groceries and literally run to get the phone before whoever was calling would hang up. If you failed to answer it, who knew when, or if, the person would call back?

All this seems silly now, but having a machine that would take a message you could play upon your return was quite an advancement for society. There were no such things as wireless phones or even cordless phones. All phones were hardwired in.

Despite this relatively advanced home office and my father's success with it, as a rule I can't ever remember him providing me much in the way of advice or guidance on either work or life, with one exception. He stressed to me that it was important that I take typing in school. Now, that was good advice and I followed it. In fact, I am benefiting from that guidance as I write this book. That's one of the few pieces of advice I can ever remember my father giving me.

My dad used to joke that he would "walk to work." By this, he meant that he would walk from the bedroom to the home office in the living room, about five steps in total. He felt this was a great advantage in that he never had to worry about traffic jams, inclement weather, car trouble, or any of the other things that come with the infamous morning and evening commute that American workers typically make. He had all the private comforts of home available to him during his work day and was able to actually get a lot of work done in the time it would have normally taken him to commute to an office.

He was smart enough to realize that it was a double-edged sword, because you can never really make a clean break from work life to home life. A "quick" detour to do something in the office before leaving for dinner could result in a two-hour delay, as one thing led to another. There was no such thing as clocking in and clocking out. Although he was his own boss, he was also responsible for everything in the business, from acquiring the clients to handling the crazed time of the year known as "tax time."

My dad's typical work day, which was seven days a week, was to get up around nine a.m., get the coffee going, and head to his desk. He would work for an hour or so, and then have a quick breakfast. He would work the rest of the morning and into mid-afternoon, at which time he would lay down and take a nap for about an hour. After getting up from the nap around four p.m., he would work another few hours until we left for a fairly late dinner, which was typically out at a restaurant. Upon returning, he would usually work another couple of hours and then sometime between eleven p.m. and midnight settle into the family room and watch some TV. Final bedtime was usually around two a.m.

Thus, he would work about 12 hours in a typical day, and generally there were no days off. This was not even during tax time. Most people work a 40-hour week, but these hours put him at around an eighty-hour work week. He seemed to enjoy the work and I never once heard him complain about it. I believe it was because he was his own boss, with his own name on the door of the business. I think he would have rather worked an eighty-hour workweek as his own boss, than a forty-hour workweek with another person to answer to.

That said, there was never really any point in time where he was fully in "relax" mode. One of the most obvious examples of that came on the night of July 20, 1969.

The country had become obsessed in the "space race" with the Soviet Union. It is impossible to really communicate what those times were like to someone who did not live through them. The specter of nuclear Armageddon was very much in people's minds, as was the concern that if the Russians could best us in space, perhaps they could do the same in many other ways of life as well.

The Mercury 7 astronauts had been tasked with getting our manned space effort under way, and they did just that. This was followed by the lesser known, but vastly important, Gemini missions, which ultimately led to the well-known Apollo era. After a series of American failures and Russian successes, the tide began to turn. America began to surpass the efforts of Russia, then known more commonly as the Soviet Union. The Apollo missions had successfully completed the groundwork for landing on the moon, and the time was right.

Michael Collins, Edwin "Buzz" Aldrin, and Neil Armstrong blasted off to the moon, with the goal of landing men on it for the first time in history. Collins would remain in the mother ship while Aldrin and Armstrong would travel down to the surface of the moon in the lunar landing module. On July 20th, they began their descent to the moon. The world and particularly Americans were utterly transfixed. Perhaps even more amazingly, we were going to watch it on TV.

Americans gathered around their televisions, and we were no exception. I was in Tucker at the time, and we had a few people over to the house. All of us, except my dad, were gathered around the TV to watch arguably the most historic event in human history. We watched as the lunar module came down to the surface of the moon after a series of adjustments by the man at the controls, Neil Armstrong.

Shortly after they landed, it was expected that Armstrong would step out onto the surface, thus becoming the first man to walk on the moon. The excitement was unbearable to an eight-year old boy like myself, but the adults were as into it as I was. Except, I noticed there was one person missing. Then, from the other room, I heard it: chuka-chuka-chuka-chuka-choo-choo-choo.

Even as a young boy I fully understood the significance of what was about to happen. I guess Pauline did too, as every once in a while she would yell out to the other room, "George, they gonna walk on the moon!" In her southern accent, George came out more like, Joe-ah-juh, but the meaning was loud and clear. The answer from the other room was always the same: "I'm coming!"

As the module door opened and Armstrong moved slowly down the ladder, her cries to George became more urgent. As George finally appeared in the room, the great Neil Armstrong took his final steps down the ladder and into history by planting his spacesuit boot on the lunar dust. For one of the few times in my life, America seemed to come together as one. George got to see it, and I'm happy about that.

However, as others sat around stunned, patriotic, proud, and joyful, knowing this was a night they would never forget as long as they lived, my father trekked back to the living room office. As the celebration continued, we heard it again: chuka-chuka-chuka-chuka-choo-choo-choo.

Even as a young boy, I must say, I felt a bit sorry for my father, who just didn't get it, but it taught me an indelible lesson about how important it is to understand the need to always place work into the right perspective. Finally, in my adult years, I was able to see Neil Armstrong speak at a conference and meet Buzz Aldrin at an event. I have a picture of Buzz and me up in *my* home office, a link to a time long ago when a little boy looked into the sky on a night when there really was a man in the moon.

14

DALE

Building tepees in the neighborhood.

When I first arrived in Tucker as a young boy, it was quite a culture shock for me. I had never really been away from my mom for any length of time, and now I was all the way across the country with my father and his new wife. I didn't know much of what to expect, but I guess I thought that since I would only be with my father for one month out of the year, he and I would spend the majority of time together doing the things that fathers and sons do. I wasn't fully clear on what those things might be though.

I learned very quickly that the father-son thing was not going to be in the equation. During my first trip there, it appeared to me that they lived exactly as they would have had I not been there, and this pattern continued throughout all the years I stayed with them during the summer.

My father would pretty much work in his home office, and Pauline would do various things around the house and occasionally head off to the "beauty parlor." When she returned, I would often ask if the beauty parlor was closed, thus endearing myself to her that much more. If you can't be a smartass when you're a kid, when can you be one?

Thus, I was left to my own devices in an unfamiliar environment. There were two things that saved me. The first was that I was a voracious reader, and fortunately had brought a lot of material with me. As a child, and even to this day, as long as I've got something good to read I can get by quite well. The second thing was Dale.

My father never took me around the neighborhood and introduced me to other families and other kids in the area. He just told me I should go outside and play. Now, at my own house, this was easy; however, in this foreign environment, I had no idea what to do when I went outside to play. I first walked around the expansive backyard and explored the creek, typically pronounced "crick." This was good for about twenty minutes. I wandered the streets but again did not have much luck. I then circled the house, which took a little while, and as I came back around to the front, I spotted another boy who appeared to be about my age. My best recollection of this encounter is that he was sitting on a storm drain at the edge of the road.

As it turned out, he lived right across the street from my father. This would have been nice to know going in, but once we met it was clear that he was in as much need of someone to play with as I was. There was utterly no way I could have known this at the time, but this first meeting was to be the beginning of what turned out to be a lifelong friendship.

Dale and I played together that summer and every summer thereafter. Many of our exploits have been detailed in other chapters, but I'll name a few here. Baseball was the sport of the season, and that was our main outdoor game. Although I loved to play football and basketball, I can't remember ever playing those sports in Tucker.

We would run loose in the neighborhood all day, unlike the highly-managed kids of today. We would float boats in the creek, fly balsa wood planes with wind-up rubber bands, have marathon games of hide-and-go-seek on my father's property, and visit other homes in the area to investigate what other activities were occurring.

I remember we came upon some kids who were building large tepees in their backyard out of huge branches. I have no idea where the branches came from, but they had a ton of them. We jumped right in and started helping them construct the tepees. Someone took a photo of all of us by the tepees, and I still have it to this day. It's hard to imagine these kinds of things happening now.

Once I got established with Dale and we brought in others from the neighborhood, things were never boring. I'm sure my father noticed that I had pretty quickly built a coalition of kids in the area, but if he was impressed with my resourcefulness, he never said so. George seemed to like Dale, who was impossible to dislike, so he was welcome to come over.

Although we were usually outside, occasionally we would take a break from the heat and humidity or from the summer rainstorms, which could appear quite suddenly. Inside our houses we made up all sorts of games, but we played many of the traditional ones as well. I particularly remember some rousing games of Candyland.

Dale was much more familiar with his house than I was with my father's, so we would spend a lot of time searching through drawers and cabinets at my place to see what we could find. Pauline had a side arrangement with an outfit known as the Vernon Company. They produced all kinds of trinkets like key chains, desk calendars, and the like. We would endlessly look through these boxes to find things we thought were interesting. I still have a ruler and a keychain from those days.

One day Dale and I were playing in my room and I determined it would be trampoline day on the bed, which had great, steel box springs. There were two beds pushed together, so you would think the logical thing for us to do would be to each jump on one of the beds. Nope. For reasons completely unclear to me then as well as now, Dale got underneath the bed.

As I jumped up-and-down as high as I could, the bed collapsed on top of Dale just as my father barreled through the door. He said, "Here, here now!" which pretty much exhausted his parenting skills. He slammed the door closed without checking on the condition of the bed or inquiring as to where Dale went. After he had left, I was able to dig Dale out of the rubble. No trip to the hospital was required, which was the definition of a good day back then.

There was also a ceramic lighter in my room that Dale was obsessed with. Each time he came over he would press the lever on this lighter, hoping to gain ignition. Over and over he would do it, each time getting a spark to appear, but no flame. This went on for many years, and he probably tried to get that lighter to go 50,000 times. I give him credit for his persistence, but since they never used that lighter, it was probably a matter of lighter fluid not being present.

Never once did he try any other solution to get it to work other than pressing the lever. I tend to think he thought that any type of action on the lighter to give it a better chance of operating would be cheating. Yes, Dale was a true purist when it came to such things. I do think that if, by a miracle, it had lit at some point, he would have passed out cold from the shock.

I believe Dale's parents had a little more trepidation about me than my father had about Dale. My father knew Dale kept me occupied, and I think that was his only real concern. Dale's parents, although happy about Dale's new playmate emerging for the summer, cast a bit more of a wary eye in my direction. In fact, in some cases you might even say it was an "evil eye."

As evening approached one day, I headed over to Dale's house. I noticed his father sitting in one of the bedrooms watching TV with the window open. The door was all the way on the other side of the house, so instead of ringing the doorbell, I walked up to the window and said, "Hi, is Dale home?"

Well, clearly his father had not seen my approach, and with my face at the screen only inches away from his in the recliner, he gave me what I described then and still describe now as the evil eye. He sized me up for a long time before he called out to Dale to tell him that I was here.

I'll never forget that expression. No one has ever looked at me that way before or since.

Another incident that gave Dale's parents pause about me was the "peanut plant" incident. As part of some school project Dale had been growing a peanut plant, which he showed to me. I have no explanation as to why I did this, but I pulled the plant out of its container. I guess you could say I was checking on the roots, but that's perhaps not the best way to help a plant thrive.

Another time when I came to Dale's front door it was open but with a screen door in place. Again it would appear my approach had been stealthy, as his mom, who was leaning way back in the recliner, did not seem to know I was at the door. The recliner was turned somewhat away from the door as I stated my usual, "Hi, is Dale home?" Since she wasn't facing me, I did not get any evil eye.

I thought it odd that as she told me that Dale wasn't home and he would be back later, she never moved an inch or even turned her head toward me. I left, but I learned later that the reason for her motionless behavior was that she was sitting in her bra and panties, trying to beat the heat. Dale's family did not indulge in air conditioning to the extent that George and Pauline did.

When Dale's parents weren't home, the activities got a bit more out-of-control. For reasons that I can't articulate at this time, one of my favorite things to do was to grab a butcher knife from the kitchen and run through the house. Even more inexplicable was that Dale would feel compelled to chase me.

On one occasion, as I ran by the dining table I knocked over a chair, which Dale promptly fell onto. I know it couldn't have possibly happened exactly like this, but my memory is of the chair being completely flattened into pieces like you would see when a cartoon character falls onto a chair and smashes it.

Upon seeing the damage to the chair, I went into the classic little-boy playbook for my response: "I've got to go now." Dale was left to glue the chair back together, and I must say my later examination revealed he did a fine job. In spite of his craftsmanship, the chair would no longer be as capable of holding weight as it originally was.

I often pictured Dale sweating bullets at their Thanksgiving meal as his stout Aunt Bertha sat on that chair, with Dale knowing it could be only seconds away from a complete collapse. Should this happen, he knew the usual suspects, mainly him, would be rounded up and questioned rigorously. By that time, I would be safely back in California, without any fear of extradition.

One of the odd quirks of Dale is that he would simply wait for my arrival in the summer. He never knew exactly when I would show up, so he would just patiently wait for me to arrive and make my trek across the street to kick off the official summer play season. He never went over to my father's house or called on the phone to inquire about when I would be arriving. He would simply wait, knowing that one day it would happen. In later years we laughed about why he never thought to find out when I would be coming to join him.

The time went by and as we got older our play rituals altered, but one thing that was a constant was that we would always be together. When we hit our later teen years and were both able to drive, that was a game-changer. We enjoyed going to the movies, and I particularly remember seeing *Jaws* and some of the *Pink Panther* movies with him.

There is a well-known amusement park in the Atlanta area known as Six Flags Over Georgia. While in my earlier years I would go with my father and Pauline, sometimes in our teens my dad would give us money and just the two of us would go. My favorite attraction was called The Great American Scream Machine, which at the time it was built was the longest, tallest, and fastest wooden roller coaster in the world. We would ride it endlessly. I'm pleased to report the coaster is still in operation, thrilling riders four-plus decades after it was built. Maybe I'll ride it again one day.

There was a custom during those times that would have been unthinkable today. Six Flags employees would roam the parking lots with Six Flags bumper stickers they would affix to your rear bumper while you were in the park. Cars in those days typically had large chrome bumpers, and bumper stickers were more common than today. What if you didn't want the sticker put on your car? Well, then you had to remember to place your sun visors down. If you didn't, you would return to your car with a fresh Six Flags bumper sticker. Imagine the reactions today if such an action were to be taken by an amusement park.

On one of these journeys to Six Flags, there was an Elvis Presley impersonator known as "Johnny C." We went to his show and it was fun, but at the level you might expect for an amusement park. We started making up stories about Johnny C., stating that he was so good the fans were beginning to treat him as if he were the real Elvis.

Adjacent to the stage was a dressing-room trailer where Johnny C. would go in between shows. We said the fans had rushed the trailer, crazed to get at Johnny C. They rocked the trailer back and forth until they turned it over and Johnny C. spilled out. These imagined stories continued to the point that we were hysterical with laughter, and even to this day I think that was one of the times I laughed the hardest and longest in my life.

Looking back on those summers I spent in Tucker, in particular the earlier ones when I was still very young, I don't know how I would have survived it without my friend Dale. He is my "brother from another mother," and Tucker without Dale would be like Nashville without music—it just wouldn't be right.

15

PLAYING IN THE NEIGHBORHOOD

Rousing games of hide-and-seek
were played in my father's backyard.

Despite the scorching heat and sweltering humidity in Tucker, we were not to be denied the outdoor pleasures of young boys. The challenges included the "chiggers." These were little, biting bugs that lay in wait in the grass and forest areas. Getting bitten up by them was just one of the occupational hazards. I didn't really know what was getting to me until the locals informed me we were in chigger territory.

I still don't know if it was really chiggers that were doing all the damage to me, but I took their word then and I'll do the same now. One of my best days in Tucker was when the "Off" bug deterrent came out. Spraying that on my legs before going out became a must.

Typically the afternoons were spent playing outside. Baseball was the main game of the summer, primarily because it was baseball season during that time. We set up our field on the side of Dale's yard, which was quite sizable. Home plate was next to the fence that enclosed their backyard. We faced the street, which was for the most part the "outfield." My father's place was across the street and only came into the equation if someone hit a stupendous shot off the bat.

I was a good athlete in all sports, and I did well in our baseball games. This is somewhat of a miracle, as I was very nearsighted. The problem was I didn't know I was nearsighted because I had nothing to compare it to. I never even gave it a thought. I just played, and played well, even though my ability to see was severely impaired. It was not until I was about nine years old that they figured out I needed glasses, but there is no doubt I needed them long before then.

In fourth-grade, our teacher would always put the answers to the math equations up on the overhead projector. For some unknown reason, she would always ask if we wanted her to read off the answers as well as display them. I would invariably scream out to read them, because I had no chance to see them from my seat. That same year they sent all of us up to the office for a hearing and eye test.

I passed the hearing test just fine, but when it came to the eye test, it didn't go so well. Looking back on it, I think the lady giving the test probably wanted to say something like, "Hey kid, you're fucked up." However, she did not say that. She merely put me on the referral list for them to call my mom and notify her that she needed to follow up on this situation.

Glasses or no glasses, I hit a moon shot one day in our baseball game. It carried over the lawn, then over the street, and then into the airspace of my father's front yard. My dad's office faced outward, and as usual, he was working at his desk. The ball just kept carrying and was straight on with a trajectory to go through the window and smack dab onto his desk. It would serve the bastard right.

Even though my sight was impaired, I knew where this ball was heading, and so did everyone else. It was like one of those slow-motion effects they do in the movies, where one of the characters says, "Nooooo" in a very slow and distorted voice. I had mixed emotions about it even as it was happening. On the one hand, my father would unquestionably be angry. There would be no mitigation based on the athleticism of the effort. If you imagine the word athlete, my dad was whatever the opposite of that word is. He cared not a whit about sports. On the other hand, the ball going through the window from that distance would have given me instant legendary status in the neighborhood.

I wish I could tell you the ball went through the window so that I could share with you a story about my dad storming out of the house and all the kids scattering, probably including me. Alas, I cannot. The ball landed in the bushes just short of the window. A tape measure shot to be sure, one which even my friend Dale fondly remembers.

The kid who lived across the street from both me and Dale was named Larry. A really good guy and a boy scout to boot. He wasn't quite the rascal that Dale and I were, but he was a big part of our network. He had a ping pong table set up in the carport, and in between baseball games we would play perpetual rounds of table tennis.

One thing that infuriated Larry was when I would hit the ping pong ball back to him without letting it bounce first. He would scream, "Let it hit the table!" This only caused me to want to do that more often. No matter how many times I did it, he still screamed the same thing over and over. I still laugh about that to this day.

As we played in the neighborhood with Larry, we knew that it was only a short matter of time until we heard his mom yell out, "Larry?"

Invariably, from wherever he was in the neighborhood, he would respond, "Ma'am?"

She would then reply, "C'mere." This would happen just about every hour on the hour, and it was always the exact same call-and-answer.

When we were engaged in long-lasting games, we always planned it to count on Larry's numerous absences. From a lesser kid we probably wouldn't have tolerated it and told him to get lost, but Larry was great and earned special dispensation.

One of our favorite games was hide-and-seek. I know to kids nowadays such a game would be laughable, but we loved it, and it was particularly fun on my father's property. One person was assigned to stay by the Cadillac in the carport, which was home base. This individual was to cover their eyes and count up to a designated number, thus giving the rest of us the time to find our hiding places. The kid who was "it" would then come to look for us. If he saw someone, he would have to run back, touch the car, and say "one, two, three," along with the person's name.

Sometimes it became a footrace back to the car. If the person looking for you got far enough away from the Cadillac, you could make a run for the carport and touch the car first, thus becoming "home free." I don't know how much fun all this sounds to you, but I can promise you that every kid that played it had a blast.

One of the techniques employed was to work in concert against the kid looking for us. On my dad's property, you could be on the front side of the house at the opposite side from the carport and see when the person came around the front looking for hiding kids. You could also station a person on the backside of the house to see if he was coming through the backyard to look for you.

Each of these people were in visual contact, so if he came around the front way or the back way, whoever had him in sight when he was far enough away from the Cadillac would run over to the other side and all of us would flee through either the front yard or the backyard to the Cadillac, while the person looking for us was on the other side of the house.

This technique was not shared with everyone who played, and a poor hapless soul named Timmy was tormented by this technique. It didn't matter if he came around the front or around the back, the other players would always be on the other side tagging the Caddie and being home free. He never figured out how we did it. Timmy, if you're reading this, now you know.

Another good one we put over on old Timmy was the time we got inside the house. Dale and I sat in my dad's office in air-conditioned comfort while Timmy padded back and forth relentlessly through the yard. At any point we could have snuck out the door to the carport and tagged home free, but we wanted to play this out for a while. We kept waiting for Timmy to glance inside the window and see us with our root beers, but it took forever. Finally he identified us from outside the window, and I wish I could describe the look on his face when he saw us. It was truly worth getting tagged out to see his expression.

Another time I got the best of my old buddy, Dale. Underneath the house was a shed, which was not quite high enough inside to stand up fully. My father kept the riding lawnmower there, along with various other yard tools. There was no lighting in this shed, only ambient light from outside when you opened the door. There was also a latch on the door. This latch could be placed horizontally, in which case the door could be pulled open with minimal force, or it could be turned vertically, so the door would stay in place and not open, either from the inside or the outside.

During one of our marathon hide-and-seek sessions, Dale got the bright idea to hide in this shed. This is not the type of shed you want to be in. Beyond the pitch-black conditions, this is exactly the kind of dark and cool place that would be sought by all kinds of creatures great and small. Nonetheless, Dale got into the shed, waiting for his chance to bolt out to the Cadillac and declare himself victorious. I was "it" for this session, and I had other ideas.

I was obviously wise to the two-man operation on the other side of the house. Although you couldn't see anyone, they could definitely be there. My countermeasure to that was to head around back at a full run, causing them to abandon their posts and go around front. Once I got about halfway into the backyard where I knew they would have already committed to the front, I would U-turn and bolt for the Cadillac, usually getting there just before them. I did this in the case at hand, but they must not have been in that location because no one took the bait.

I then moved around the backyard more methodically. As I passed the shed, I twisted the latch so the door wouldn't open. I didn't know if anyone was in there or not, but if they were, I wanted to control when they came out. It took a long time to eventually ferret out the other hiders, and then I noticed Dale was not in the mix.

I had forgotten about the shed. No doubt by this time he had been screaming to get out, but no one could hear him because the loud air conditioning unit was right next to the shed. I went to the shed and threw the door open. Out stumbled Dale, who at that point was no threat to bolt for the Cadillac. It reminded me of the scene in *The Sixth Sense* where the kid gets locked in a compartment with ghosts and goes absolutely bonkers. This was Dale's version of that scene. Let's just say no one was ever tempted to hide in the shed again.

There was another boy in the neighborhood named Johnny. He was a bit on the chubby side and was not in the "sharpest tool in the bin" category. He decided one day that he was going to hide in the storm drain. This was not a good idea for a multitude of reasons. With Johnny's girth, squeezing into the storm drain was difficult, and you know for sure that getting out was going to be even more difficult.

There were two ways you could get into the storm drain. First, was to lower yourself into it at the street level. Second, you could crawl into the outlet, which was about halfway down the slope of my dad's backyard. Johnny chose the latter, which was the better choice.

At some point, he thought he would get cute and instead of just hiding at the edge of the storm drain until the coast was clear, he decided to crawl all the way through the storm drain and come out on the street side. What possessed him to do this I'll never know, but that's what he did. What could go wrong?

Well, what could go wrong did go wrong, and Johnny was stuck in the storm drain. We figured out he was in there by his screams for help, which I will tell you did not sound John Wayne-ish in any way. At first we thought, "Oh my God, there's a little girl stuck in the storm drain screaming for help." We figured out pretty quickly it was Johnny. We managed to fish him out of there without calling for rescue equipment, but it was a close one. I didn't really care too much that Johnny got stuck. By the time we got him out of there the game had broken up, and I hold him fully responsible for ruining the fun that day for everyone. An unforgiveable transgression according to the "kids' code."

In any event, I am willing to bet that those of us who played that game on my father's property remember it very well and very happily. I know I do, as is the case with all of our other games. I wish we could do it all again, but I guess that's not in the cards. It may not have been Paris, as in the movie *Casablanca,* but nonetheless, all of us kids will always have Tucker.

16

THE ROCK

Rocky, my "lifetime" dog.

Like most people, I've had quite a few pets over the years, but there was only one that was my "lifetime" dog. Animal people know right away what I mean by such a statement, but for the uninitiated, this means that out of all the pets you've had in your life there is usually one that stands above the others, your lifetime pet. For me, this was Rocky, who came to be mine when I was a young boy and was often affectionately known as "The Rock."

Rocky was designated as a collie-shepherd mix, but the truth may have been closer to "uncertain origin." I got Rocky at the Humane Society for the princely sum of $16, surely the best money I have ever spent in regard to return investment. Rocky was listed as a male, which influenced the name I chose, after the popular movie character of the time. The first trip to the vet revealed that Rocky was, in fact, a female.

Despite her newfound status as a girl, the name stuck. Rocky was only a few months old when I got her, and like a lot of other "pound mutts," she was whip-smart, much more so than the other pedigreed dogs that later became part of our family.

One of those pedigreed animals was a sheepdog named Binky. He had a lot of heart but was not really the brains of the operation. He did have the distinction of being the main player in one of the funnier incidents that occurred in our home. I was really sick and was laying on the couch in the living room when the doorbell rang. My brother was home and I told him to answer the door and get rid of whoever it was, because I was too ill.

We had one of those security screen doors where you can see out, but people on the porch can't really see in. My brother opened the wood door, leaving the screen door closed. As it turned out, it was a Cub Scout who was selling tickets for the Scout Jamboree. He made his pitch through the screen door, despite being unable to see the person who answered. As he finished, Binky came bounding up and tried to muscle his way past my brother and get out the door. The Cub Scout was not able to see this happening. My brother says to the Scout, "No," meaning we were not interested in any tickets.

Following very closely on that no, he said to Binky in a very loud voice, "Get out of here!" Well, all the scout heard in response to his sales pitch was, "No, get out of here!" He took off like a shot, and my brother closed the door, not realizing how what he said had sounded to the boy. I did, however, and even in my sickened condition I fell on the floor laughing.

It took me a few minutes of choking and wheezing to get it out, but when I finally explained to my brother how it must have sounded to the scout, he, too, became hysterical. We laughed the rest of the afternoon about it. We have been laughing about it ever since, and occasionally in response to something that has occurred, one of us will say, "No, get out of here!" Binky was a Hall of Famer on that one alone.

Rocky was a very sweet-natured dog, who quickly won over everyone in the family. Even my grandmother, who usually put a lot of space between herself and any dog, was taken with her. I grew up with Rocky, and she was very much a part of my young life.

Rocky loved to eat, as do most dogs. I could pitch her a piece of steak or other such food, and her ability to catch it in her mouth was quite remarkable. I honestly can't remember her dropping any food I threw her way. I used to love those "all you can eat" rib nights at restaurants because I would sneakily bring home a full beef rib for The Rock. There were quite a few times when she didn't even wait for the food to be thrown or given.

There was the time I was eating chicken on the bed in my room, specifically a drumstick. I was engrossed in watching a sporting event on TV, and as usual, Rocky was up on the bed with me. I paused in eating the chicken leg because of the excitement of what was on TV and held it in my hand off to the side. When there was a break in the action, I went back to eating my chicken, but there was only the handle part of the drumstick left.

Evidently while I was transfixed with the sporting event, Rocky had bit it in two. I grabbed it back out of her mouth as I did not want her to choke on it and then pieced it off to her. You might think I'm exaggerating. How could the dog bite the drumstick in half without me realizing it? That was the smarts of Rocky; she bit it off so gently I didn't even notice.

In another instance, my mom was preparing steaks for dinner. When Rocky wanted to go outside, she would go to the back door and wait for one of us to open it. When my mom let Rocky out, she seemed to notice something odd about her, but couldn't quite put her finger on it. When she returned to making dinner, the three steaks she had, had been reduced to two steaks. She then realized Rocky looked odd because her mouth was so full.

My favorite incident was when my brother made a large plate of ham cold cuts and cheese. At the time, he lived in the apartment we had above the main house. He would often come down and raid the refrigerator. As he was making his way back to the stairs, we met up and I told him I wanted to show him something in the den. He put his plate down on a bench that was about a foot off the ground.

A couple of minutes later we returned, but it was clear that the plate was not quite as full as when we had left. There was no sign of Rocky when he had put the plate down, nor was there any sign of Rocky when we returned.

Now most dogs would have just eaten the whole thing and been done with it. However, both of us believed, knowing Rocky, that she had tried to calculate how much she could eat without being noticed. And no, it wasn't that she got full; Rocky really didn't have a "full" button when it came to eating. Even my brother had to laugh about that one. You have to give a dog that thinks so strategically a break.

Rocky was a beloved companion throughout my youth. You know the story, though, as a boy grows up school, jobs, and social events begin to take more and more time. The day came for me to move into my own home, and I debated whether to take Rocky with me. Wanting her to be around and caring for her was no problem, but with going to college and working, she would have been at my new house by herself most of the time.

Knowing that my mom would be home all day, and Rocky would have the company of her and the other dogs, I chose to let Rocky continue to live at my mom's house. I would only be living, working, and going to college ten minutes or so away from the house, so I would be able to visit all the time. I brought her over to my house on weekends when I could.

One of the most difficult things with pets is that you can't explain things to them. Rocky certainly knew that things had changed, but she had to import her own meaning to it. I think if I could have one of those "superpowers," other than maybe turning invisible at will, I would choose to be able to talk to animals. That would have certainly come in handy in explaining the situation to her.

At the time, I had a Chevrolet Camaro. Whenever I would drive up in front and Rocky would hear that car, she would get up on two legs and start violently rocking the back screen door so my mom would let her in. My mom said she always knew when it was my car; there were never any false alarms. Smart dog.

Rocky aged well and was fifteen-years old before I knew it. Although she had lost a bit of hearing, she seemed to be in good health for a dog of that age. She never really had any physical problems throughout her life. As she got older, it did cross my mind that her natural lifespan was drawing near, but it was a thought that was just too disturbing to dwell on.

The call came from my mom on a Saturday afternoon. "Rocky's sick," she said. I had just been over to the house and she seemed fine, but when I returned, I found a different dog. She perked up when I arrived but was obviously ailing. She walked a few steps and collapsed with some sort of seizure.

We took her to the vet and the diagnosis was a heart ailment. The doctor said that if Rocky were a human being, the remedy would be the placement of a pacemaker to regulate her heart rhythm. The alternative for dogs was medication. She stayed at the vet for a few days. We brought home a very sick dog.

We gave medication to her, but one of the biggest problems was that she did not have an appetite. She was alert and seemed to understand that a change had occurred in her body. I remember sitting on the floor next to her and having a tear land on the back of my hand. She moved over and licked it off.

We kept vigil over her, hoping that the medication would kick in and improvement would occur. If it did not, decision time was nearing and I had to be the one to make it. Although she didn't seem to be in any obvious pain, her quality of life had become very poor. She would continue to weaken if we could not get her to eat. I wished for a sign of the right thing to do, but I knew in my heart there would be no magic answer.

After spending a great deal of time with Rocky for about a week after her return from the animal hospital, I became convinced of several things. First, despite her gentle nature, Rocky was, like her namesake, a fighter, and would not give up. Second, the medication was not working and her discomfort appeared to be increasing. Third, I believed there was an animal equivalent of dignity, just as with human beings, and Rocky was close to losing that due to her condition.

The ride to the vet's office was a difficult one. I carried Rocky in my arms to the examination room. The doctor confirmed what we already knew, and I gave him the authorization to do what needed to be done.

I began to say my goodbyes to my old friend, but eyes can sometimes communicate more than words, especially between humans and animals. My eyes and hers communicated the many years of love and companionship. I believe in her mind she knew it was time to let go. I think we were both grateful we were together in her final days.

The end came swiftly, and I hope and believe, painlessly. I held her in my arms and cried. The image of her on the table will stay with me the rest of my life. Despite this, I wouldn't have done it any other way. Rocky and I began our journey together, and it was only right that we end it together. I felt it was my duty to comfort her through this final act. However, I would never criticize a pet owner who could not stand to be in the room when it occurred. This is a very personal decision, but for me, it was the only one, and I've never regretted it.

Euthanasia is supposed to be a painless death designed to bring about a peaceful end to one's suffering, and I am sure that is what occurred in Rocky's case. Ironically, for me, it was quite a painful process, even though I know I did right by her.

There is a grieving process that occurs with both human loss and the loss of a beloved pet. I would never be one to equate the two, but I think there are some similarities. I've heard it said that the stages of grief occur for the loss of a pet just as with a human, but that it typically moves through the stages faster for a beloved pet. Having grieved both pets and human loved ones, I think maybe there is something to this.

It has been well over 20 years since I lost Rocky. I still have dreams about her at times, and do I ever love her up during those very realistic dreams. They say that a person dies, but the relationship continues. I think that is how it is with Rocky. I still feel she is part of my life and always will be. I sure loved that dog. I hope I get to see her again.

17

PEAPOD

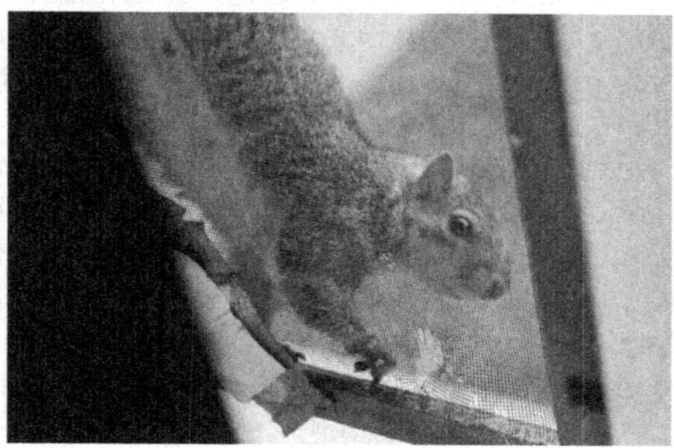

Peapod on the screen waiting for walnuts.

After Rocky, I never had much of a heart for getting new pets. I think the loss of her was too much to bear and caused me to not want to have to go through that loss again. I think maybe "on paper" that's understandable, but I know that in life this may be a form of shortsighted thinking. Although I didn't adopt too many other pets in the years after Rocky was gone, a rather strange thing happened.

There were some crazy critters who decided to adopt me. Before I tell that tale, I must tell you about the tree. Most all of the stories in this memoir focus on my young existence, but this will be my one major divergence into my adult life.

I first saw the big oak tree almost 30-years ago, and it was probably 80 years old at that time. As trees go, there is something special about an oak. I couldn't help but notice how magnificent it looked in the front yard of the house for sale. I loved the neighborhood and the home, but perhaps most of all I loved the tree. I bought the house and became the "owner" of the tree, although I suppose no one ever really owns something of such magnificence. Perhaps "caretaker" or "custodian" is a better description of what my role was to be.

About 15 years into my ownership of the property, the leaves on the oak tree turned brown almost overnight. An arborist came out and informed me the tree had died, victimized by an oak root fungus that such trees were susceptible to. The news just about caused my knees to buckle. The arborist explained that a tree will continue to use up all of its reserves, keeping the tree looking normal until almost the very end. Then, the reserves run out, and the visible changes that indicate death occur very rapidly.

I thought of what the tree had meant to me over the years and couldn't help but think of Shel Silverstein's well-known parable, *The Giving Tree.* One of the things that makes that book so unique is that everyone seems to have their own interpretation of the true meaning of the story. The message I got from the book was that we should be kind and grateful to those things that give much to us, even if they make no such demands in return.

The tree gave much to me. It shaded my whole house during the hot summers. It provided a daily dose of beauty and character to the place in which I lived. The tree was also home to various creatures, most notably a large number of squirrels. I had enjoyed their perpetual antics, even if it did sound like a herd of elephants as they scampered across the roof.

The only thing squirrels are loyal to is a consistent food source, and with the loss of the tree they would be moving on. They scattered like crazy when I came out the front door, but I still got a lot out of watching their hijinks. In addition to missing my beloved tree, I would miss them.

We live in a pretty urban area, but that doesn't stop the wildlife from coming to visit. Over the years, in addition to the squirrels, we've had birds, hawks, wild parrots, raccoons, skunks, possums, rabbits, lizards, coyotes, and perhaps most surprisingly, peacocks.

After a while, I noticed the squirrels had returned, but primarily to the backyard. For reasons unknown to me, they seemed to be a little less frightened of me in the backyard as opposed to the front yard. Unlike the front yard, in the backyard there is patio furniture, which has a covering over the white stuffing inside the cushions.

One day, from inside the house, I noticed a squirrel up on the patio furniture. When the squirrel looked up, she looked like a Santa Claus squirrel. She had torn open the cushion covering and removed a large chunk of the stuffing. It looked like she had a huge white beard. She scampered off with the stuffing, no doubt using it to make a Ritz Carlton-level squirrel nest.

I don't know how she surmised there would be fluffy material beneath the much harder cushion covering. She was clearly intending on building a nest, so we christened her "Mama Squirrel." She came back quite a few times to get sufficient material, and we figured we should wait until after the nesting season to replace our cushions.

Intrigued by Mama Squirrel, I began leaving a little food out for her, which she happily took, eating some and taking some back to the nest. Over time, some other squirrels showed up, and I started feeding them as well. This has gone on for many years now and has developed into an almost unbelievable routine. Many squirrels have come and gone, but we always have some around.

Even to this day, there are several who come to visit with us, usually once in the morning and once in the late-afternoon. These critters have become our pets to some degree, just without the normal responsibilities. I want to tell you about some of them, and I'll begin with the most special one of all, one we named "Peapod."

We suspect Peapod may have been the offspring of Mama Squirrel, due to the timing of her arrival and her quick comfort level with me. After observing and interacting with these critters over many years, I can tell you that their personalities and intellect vary greatly. Peapod was an extremely smart squirrel, who was able to "train" me in pretty short order.

Normally I would see Peapod out in the backyard and I would go out and feed her, which typically consisted of throwing her walnuts or shelled peanuts from a distance. I came to believe Peapod's nest wasn't too far away, as she would often show up when I went out to the backyard. She even took to sitting on the apex of my back neighbor's roof, which had a perfect sightline to the backdoor I would use to exit the house. After a while, I could feed her on the neighbor's roof by simply throwing a walnut or peanut up there. She would eat one and wait for the next one to be thrown.

Squirrels are inherently afraid of humans, whom they see as potential threats. Nonetheless, Peapod rapidly began to get more and more comfortable around me. I think squirrels are much like people, in that their level of trust in you dictates how they behave around you. The squirrels who didn't "know" me would take off immediately when I came outside. Peapod, on the other hand, would run toward me, as she had determined I was not a threat and that I always had a tasty treat for her.

Eventually, Peapod searched for a more efficient way of getting me to feed her, instead of simply waiting for me to come out. There is a wooden screen door that leads to the backyard. Peapod deduced that if she climbed up on that door and rattled it, it would get my attention, and it did. I typically sit in a recliner by that door, and you always knew when Peapod arrived.

As this continued, Peapod became so comfortable with me that I could easily feed her by hand. Now, don't try this at home. This was only done after a very long period of acclimation, and even then it probably wasn't the best idea, but after a while it seemed right to both me and her. We developed a routine where I would sit on the back porch and she would put her front paws on my leg and take her walnut or peanut. She would get down, eat that one, and return, and this would go on until she was full. People who came over and saw this ritual were astonished.

Other squirrels would come around as well and I would feed them too, but no other squirrel was like Peapod in their comfort with me. It is very unusual for a skittish creature like a squirrel to not be tense around humans, but Peapod got to the point that you could tell she was very relaxed around me. This ritual went on for a long time, and eventually,

Peapod had babies, and she brought them down to be fed and to train them on the food routine.

They don't coddle the babies too much in the squirrel world. I remember putting some food down on the tile area of the barbeque for Peapod and her young one. I thought the little one would eat, followed by Peapod, but not so. Peapod ate first until she got her fill, and the baby waited. When he had the nerve to try and sneak a bite before she had finished, he got slapped in the face, and no, I'm not making that up. Having learned his lesson, he then was allowed to eat once Peapod was done.

You'll never see two adult squirrels eating at the same food pile. It is always a question of who will be dominant, and that one will eat. This results in constant face-offs and duke-outs. Nothing too serious. It's just the way it is.

One of the most interesting scraps I saw was between a squirrel that was very comfortable with me and another who was not. As I was sitting on the back porch step, they went at each other. I stood up to break up the fight, and as I did, the one that was comfortable with me ran over at full speed toward me. He stopped right at my feet, turned to face the direction of his opponent and got up on his two hind legs. The other squirrel looked at him in what I can only classify as disbelief and ran off. I know it's hard to believe, but there is no doubt in my mind that "my" squirrel had run to me for protection.

Peapod was always my favorite, but over time I became quite comfortable with many others. I noticed one day Peapod was up on the barbeque and one of her rear legs had been badly injured, perhaps broken. The other squirrels were harassing her, which I came to learn is what occurs at any sign of weakness.

I got what later became known as my "squirrel stick," and kept the marauders at bay by placing the stick between them and me. These were squirrels who were not frightened of me, and they would often grab at the stick with curiosity. One even tried to make off with it when I set it down on the grass. I kept Peapod up on the barbeque and brought her some food and a small container of water. She ate and drank while I worked security.

This pattern repeated itself for many days. I could hear her slowly make her way down in the bushes toward the barbeque. I couldn't put the food and water down until she got there because the other squirrels would have poached it. Once she arrived, I gave her the food and water. She would eat one big batch and take a long drink of water. She would eat a second batch and take a second drink of water. Then she would slowly make her way back up the bushes, presumably to her nest. Eventually, she recovered and returned to our usual feeding pattern. Peapod was "my" squirrel for a long time.

I found her in the street one day, having suffered the fate of many a squirrel—hit by a car. I am hoping that death was quick. I knew right away it was her. She now resides in her rightful place in the backyard, marked by a small stone marker. I still miss her.

People often ask me if I can tell the squirrels apart. The answer is yes, but not in the way you would think. Sure, sometimes there are obvious markings that make them distinctive, but most of the time I tell them apart by their behavior. They all behave differently around me, depending on how much they've come to trust me, which can vary a great deal. However, once a given squirrel decides to trust me, they don't seem to have the need to ever revisit that decision.

Another squirrel that was one of my favorites was "Picky Bicky," so named because of his discerning food preferences. Picky was both a "screen climber," meaning he knew to get on the back screen to get our attention and get fed, and a "hand feeder," meaning that both of us trusted each other enough to allow that behavior to occur. Most squirrels will eat whatever you give them, but not Picky.

Occasionally Picky would eat a peanut, but more often than not he preferred shelled walnuts. During such times, if you held out a peanut for him to take, he would do what we came to call a "nose bump." Meaning, he would bump the peanut with his nose instead of taking it. This was your signal to replace the peanut with a walnut, which he would then happily take. Although Peapod would occasionally do this, Picky was the only one to do it on a consistent basis. I am sad to report that Picky met the same fate as Peapod, both in the cause of death and resting place.

Sometimes people ask me if I ever let them in the house, and the answer is no. Although I am comfortable interacting with the squirrels in the way I described, letting them in the house doesn't feel right to me. They are wild creatures, and that's a boundary I think should stay in place. I can promise you though, if I gave them a chance they would do it in a heartbeat. I often have to block them with my foot when I open the screen door to keep them from barging in.

I have several squirrels at the present time who are regulars. One in particular has adopted the behavior of getting up on the patio cushions and looking into the house to get our attention. He will make direct eye contact with us as we sit in the room we call the "clubhouse." I can also "call" certain squirrels. When I open the door in the morning and make a noise they recognize, if they are within earshot, they will usually be rattling the screen door within several minutes. This advancement has led to a real ease in accomplishing the feeding task.

Perhaps the squirrel I've grown fondest of lately is named "Chunktail." She has been part of my crew for a long time. She was named this because, evidently, she got into it with somebody who took a huge chuck out of her bushy tail. It has never grown back, thus making her easy to identify. She is a regular on the screen door and will also run over to me when I "call" her. Her latest trick is to climb up on my sweatpants as she waits for me to drop some walnuts. We're not quite at the Peapod level of trust yet, but it's gotten pretty close.

If years ago someone had told me that I would be having squirrels rattle my screen door to get my attention, take food from my hand, make eye contact with me from the outside patio chairs, and come when I call them, I'd have said you were out of your mind. Yet, that is exactly what happened and continues to happen to this day. I'll grant you that this is pretty weird stuff, but my family and I have had an endless amount of fun and entertainment from our little backyard friends, all for the price of some walnuts. A pretty good deal, wouldn't you say?

18

THE KING

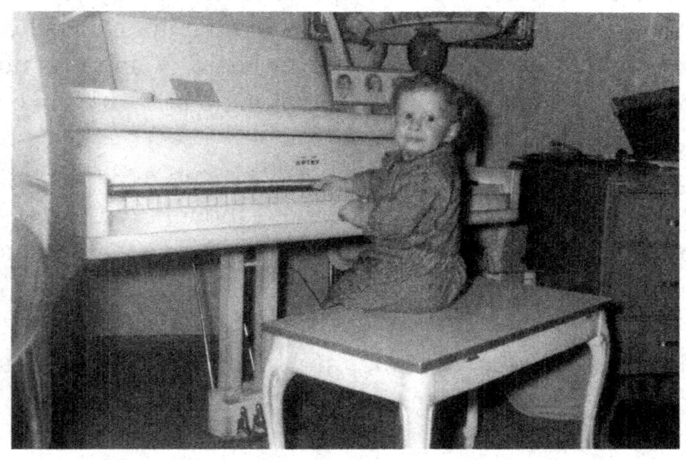

Musical talent being displayed early on.

I was often told by my parents that when I was a baby, there was one particular song that, when it came on the radio, would cause me to go nuts. It was called, *The Lion Sleeps Tonight*, by The Tokens. You may not know the name of the song, but you've certainly heard it before: "We dee dee dee dee dee dee dee dee dee wee umm umm a laaayyyy, a wing a whet a wing a whet a wing a whet a wing a whet a wing a whet a wing a whet a wing a whet a wing a whet…" I guess I've always had a love of music.

I even became a "professional" musician in later life. I had always played around on the drums, but when I retired, I took it up more seriously. I joined a band and played some paid gigs, thus the somewhat tongue-in-cheek reference to being a professional musician. The first time I played with a band was at a music studio.

The band, called Last Train, had a drummer who wasn't working out, and they asked me to sit in with them to see if I might be a good fit. Although I had played drums extensively at home, it was confined to playing along with a CD with headphones on. Don, the leader of the group, gave me a CD of familiar rock and blues songs and said these would be the songs we would play at our first rehearsal.

As this would be my first time actually playing live with other musicians, I wanted to be well prepared. I practiced diligently to that CD and was ready to go for our first practice. After setting up, Don called off the first song we would do, which I had never heard of and was not on the CD he gave me. So there I was, playing along on the drums to a song I knew nothing about.

I expected at some point for them to just stop and look at me, but they didn't, so I kept playing at a pace that I thought felt right. After the song had ended, I thought maybe they just used it as a warm-up song and that they just fooled around as they played. Now we would get to the real songs on the CD.

Don called off the second song, and again it was one I had never heard of. Off we went, with me playing like crazy to a song I didn't know. Again, no one said anything to me or looked at me funny. I was further observing to see if they were exchanging odd glances with each other, but nothing.

After this song, I asked Don if we would play any of the songs on the CD he gave me, and he said, "Oh, yeah." We then played a song I knew, and I felt better. I may not have played great, but at least I knew what the song was supposed to sound like.

The next song was *Taking Care of Business*, by Bachman-Turner Overdrive. This song had been on the CD and was one I knew even before that, so it went pretty well. That is, until we got to a "break" in the song, and Don said, "Take it." He wasn't looking at anyone in particular when he said it, but even as a novice I knew what it meant. Someone was going to do a solo. I was excited to see this, and I tapped quietly in rhythm until I figured out who was going to do the solo, at which point I would cease to play altogether.

I don't know how much time went by, but there was a point that came where it dawned on me that this solo was a drum solo. No one made any prior mention of this to me. I then improvised what may have been the worst drum solo in the history of music. It wasn't my fault though; it was a set up.

Ultimately we ended up playing quite a few street fairs and other events, and I think we did pretty well. One thing is for sure though, the next time we played *Taking Care of Business,* I had a solo ready that would knock you out.

Going back to my younger days, when I was about seven-years old I had a few of my own records. Of course, there was no such thing as Apple's iTunes® or even compact discs at that time. For those youngsters reading this, records were played on a phonograph, which had a needle that was placed on the record and into the grooves. Nostalgic types now call these pieces of ancient history "vinyl."

I specifically remember one record by Bill Haley and the Comets called, *See You Later Alligator.* As I listened to this record, I would typically shout out the line after the title of the song: "After while crocodile." These songs were nice, but I was about to experience a lightning bolt.

My brother had left behind some records when he moved on from the house, and I began flipping through them. One particular album, as they were called in those days, caught my eye. There was a very handsome, smiling young singer on the front. It seemed as if his face took up the entire cover. I had no idea if I would like the songs, but I figured I'd give it a shot.

I didn't know it at the time, but when I put that record on it was to be the beginning of a lifelong relationship, one that is now almost fifty-years old—a relationship that was highlighted by actually visiting this singer's house, although, sadly, he was not there at the time. The young man's name was Elvis Presley.

Elvis hooked me right from the start. It was clear to me then and it's clear to me now that he was unique in voice, but it turned out there was much more. Elvis was known as "The King of Rock and Roll," but now it's most often simply, "The King." This was not a self-initiated nickname, like Michael Jackson's "King of Pop." This was a name bestowed on him by the people.

He achieved worldwide fame, but his status in the South far surpasses even that. As my parents hailed from the South, he was revered like no other. I think in part because they saw much of themselves in him. He was just a dirt-poor country boy who happened to make it big, but they still considered him "one of us."

If you were to view an Elvis concert film, you would notice an incredible range of ages in the audience, unlike almost any other entertainer. This was the case in my house as well, as his appeal spanned several generations. My grandmother was as much a fan as I was, and like a lot of people in the South, she pronounced his name "Evalis." When he died in 1977, our whole family grieved.

Only forty-two years of age when he left us, but what a life. Everyone talked about how tragic it was for him to die so young, but there was an earlier girlfriend of his that had a different take. She said she thought that Elvis lived about as long as he wanted. This struck me as odd at first, but the more I've thought about it, the more it seems to make some sense to me. Aging is difficult for all of us, but how very difficult it must be for someone who made a name for himself so young. It got me to thinking that maybe everyone is not destined for a long life, even if their genetics would allow for it.

One day shortly after my admiration for Elvis began, I was over at our family friends, the Harrington's. I excitedly told the matriarch of that family of my new favorite singer. She went to a drawer in the kitchen and returned with a color photo of Elvis. It was autographed, and it was my understanding at the time that it was an actual autograph, not one of those commonplace "autopen" type signatures. I was quite taken aback when I learned it was her intention to give it to me. As you might imagine, I treasured that photo, but unfortunately, I didn't get a chance to treasure it for long.

Sometime after I returned home with my photo, my brother stopped by as he would do from time to time. I made the huge mistake of showing him my gift. He said it was quite nice and then asked if he could have it. As I've explained in earlier chapters, because he was so much older than me, the request was more as if a parental-type authority figure had made it. I reluctantly said, "Okay," and that was that. I don't know how long that picture remained in his possession, but if typical form held true, probably not long, and it was in all likelihood given to a girl with "beautiful eyes."

About 45 years later, I was having a conversation with some of the Harringtons at a holiday dinner. I explained I was writing a childhood memoir and told them the story of how their mother had given me the autographed picture of Elvis and how I no longer possessed it. I told them I had the impression that the autograph on the photo was actually inscribed by Elvis himself.

They told me about a family member during that time who worked at a film studio where Elvis frequently made movies. It was not uncommon for this family member to encounter Elvis. They were firmly convinced it was an actual autographed photo. I wasn't sure whether to laugh or cry when they told me this, but I pass it on for the reader's consideration.

Don't feel too bad for me. I've recovered quite well and have accumulated a very nice collection of Elvis memorabilia. I have signed eight-by-ten concert photos, a personalized guitar pick he played with in concert, and one of the cufflinks given to him by President Nixon when he visited the White House. I occasionally take them out of storage to look at them, and I really enjoy having these items.

I have these in addition to all the other things you might expect, like large audio and video collections. I have two fireplaces in my home, and over each one is a painting of Graceland, Elvis' home, done by the famous artist Thomas Kinkade. One is a scene of the home in the springtime and one at Christmas.

The Christmas one particularly stands out in our household. As in many homes, there is often something that occurs that is considered the "official" kick off of the Christmas season. At our place, it's me playing the Elvis Christmas CD my wife got for me many years ago. Despite all this, I still wish I had that first picture.

My brother was responsible for something else with a link to Elvis. He was a musician at various times, and as with a lot of things in his life, musical ventures were not always done in a low-key way. It was always a "moon shot" with my brother. There was a time when I was an adult still living in the family home, and he had taken up residence in the study of the house.

It was a bit of an odd setup, in that I had to pass through the study to get to my quarters. He had his own landline phone in that room, and it wasn't uncommon for me to answer the phone if he wasn't around. My brother had mentioned to me that he was considering putting a band together, but I didn't pay much attention as this was somewhat of a perpetual situation.

I should tell you first that I was a big fan not only of Elvis but of his concert band, who I still feel are one of the best backing bands ever. In particular, I admired Ronnie Tutt, the drummer, but I also liked James Burton, the guitar player. By this time, Elvis was gone, but his band continued on as working musicians for many other artists.

One day my brother's phone rang, and without thinking I picked it up. The person on the other end asked for him, and because he wasn't there, I asked who was calling. He said, "Ronnie Tutt." I don't know how much time passed, but I believe it was quite a bit.

I then said, "*The* Ronnie Tutt?"

He said, "Yeah, I think so." I then went on to have a nice conversation with, in my opinion, one of the best big band rock and roll drummers who ever lived. I ultimately realized that when my brother was talking about "getting a band together," he was talking about Elvis' old band. Only Bubba…

When my brother returned, he got the message that Ronnie Tutt had called, and an earful from me for not giving me adequate warning that he might call so I wouldn't sound like an awestruck teenager. However, this story tells you a lot about my brother. Of course, this "band" never got off the ground, but it sure was fun to talk to Ronnie. Later, I fielded a call from James Burton on the same line, and believe you me, I was cool, calm, and collected for that one.

One of my few regrets in life was that I did not get to see Elvis live in concert. I was only sixteen when he died, so it would have been difficult for me to pull off a trip to Las Vegas by myself to see him in the early seventies when I was only ten or so. There was family talk over the years about doing it, but it never happened. By the time I was old enough to make it occur on my own, he was gone.

I did get an opportunity to see a show called "Elvis: The Concert" in 1998 at Radio City Music Hall in New York. In this show, they had put together all of Elvis' touring band from Las Vegas. Yes, including my old friends Ronnie and James.

This huge band, with full orchestra and multiple backing vocal groups, took the stage and played live as Elvis sang on the giant screen. They had taken the vocals from his concerts, isolated them, cleaned them up with digital technology, and synchronized them to the live playing of his old band. It looked and sounded like a real concert, and he even introduced the band members on stage—twenty years after his death. I've never seen anything like it, and for me, it was a very emotional experience. Not the same as seeing the man himself, but certainly as close as I'll ever get.

I made the required pilgrimage to Graceland in Memphis, Tennessee in 1988, which was also a very moving experience. There are not too many famous people who could draw so many visitors to their house long after they've been gone.

When I visited, there was a grouping of buildings across the street from the home, along with a staging area for the minibuses that would carry visitors across the highway to the house for the tour. As you might imagine, there were souvenirs galore, but sweatshirts and shot glasses were not the mementos I was after. What I wanted was a picture of myself standing in front of Graceland, with the entire house in the background. Easy, you say? Well, perhaps if you weren't too picky, but I wanted a photo of myself in front of Graceland *with no one else visible* in the picture. Not so easy.

The tour buses drove in and out of the gates constantly, dropping off people to enter the front door of the house and picking people up after they had finished the tour. After arriving on site, I studied the operation for a while and concluded my objective was difficult, but not impossible. Like many things in life, it was an issue of timing. When the buses pulled up and unloaded the people, they would line up and begin entering the house, but typically, before they finished entering, there would be another bus arriving with more people, thus messing up the picture I had in mind.

After waiting through numerous cycles of this, there finally came a time where just as the front door was closing and there was another bus coming up the driveway, there was about one second to get a picture. It's now an eight-by-ten beauty up on the wall in my office. The arriving bus was just a couple of feet from entering the frame as the front door closed, but you'd never know it from looking at the picture. It simply looks like I was able to stand in front of Graceland on a day they were closed to the public. I guess most good pictures have stories behind them.

Like it is for many of his fans, Elvis will be a part of my life until the day I die. In my biased view, he was the greatest entertainer who ever lived. There are not too many people who are at the head of the line when it comes to handing out talent, looks, and charisma, but for whatever reason, he was the guy. I think my grandmother summed it up best in something she repeated many times: "There'll never be another one like him." Long live The King.

19

THE TRAVELING TV

An early family predecessor of the Traveling TV.

It is my desire in writing this memoir to keep things relatively light, yet true in spirit. Thus I must tell you the story of the Traveling TV. It is admittedly not my most pleasant childhood memory, but it has its place in the book because it reveals so much about my brother Bubba, my father George, and my position in the pecking order during those days.

The sixties were a very different time for raising children as compared to today. The popular show *Mad Men* did a good job of portraying this. Back then, almost all homes were what I would call "parent-centered." Meaning, the focus of what went on in the home was on the parents. Children were meant to be seen and not heard—and not even seen that much.

Parents did what they wanted to do, and children took a back seat. To be told to keep quiet and go to your room was a mantra that was common. It's not that parents didn't love their children. They did. However, they didn't let children drive everything, as is often the case now. When I got pesky as a child, my mom used to tell me to go play on the freeway, but that was a joke—I think.

Today, homes seem to be more "child-centered," meaning the child takes center stage and the parents revolve around them rather than the other way around. The term "helicopter parent" has emerged to describe mothers and fathers constantly hovering over their children in a way that was not the case in the past. This hovering is physical in some cases, but extends beyond that via technology.

This stems in part from the parents' desire to feed their child's self-esteem, something that has become somewhat of a divinity to parents. "Yes, Johnny, your award for most improved camper is absolutely equal to someone winning an Olympic gold medal. You're special." This "special" proclamation occurs regardless of the actual merits of the child's performance or behavior. High self-esteem, however unwarranted it may be, is considered vital at all costs. This is the goal regardless of any other factors. It is believed by these parents that this high self-esteem will lead to extraordinary outcomes in raising their children.

It is well beyond the scope of this memoir to get into the unintended consequences of raising children this way, but you can see the results on a daily basis as kids run recklessly through restaurants and stores, with parents scared to death to put a stop to it—it might hurt their self-esteem. Parents have become very good at relentlessly blustering threats of punishment that are never carried out. Children, understandably so, have learned not to pay any attention to this, and they act accordingly.

I recently witnessed an instance that epitomized this. I was in the post office and there was a mother there with three children, and they were completely wild. So much so that customers in line and postal clerks were exchanging glances, hoping, to no avail, that the mother would take action. Her "action" consisted of warnings, threats, and the all-time classic of counting to ten. The idea being the child was allowed to continue misbehaving until she reached ten.

This lady could have counted to a million and nothing was going to happen. Her words were simply not backed by actions. This is a bad strategy from parenting all the way to running countries. These children were some of the worst behaved I've ever seen, and believe me, that's saying something.

That's not the "kicker," though. As I walked out of the post office, this mother was loading her charges into the proverbial minivan, and I was close enough to her to hear what she was saying. She was telling them that she was going to take them for ice cream because of how well they had behaved in the post office.

I've digressed a bit, but I wanted to paint some context between how parents handled children in the sixties versus now. For those of you around during those times, I have no doubt you are nodding your head in agreement with what I am saying. For those of you who were not around during those times, I think it is important for you to know that things were very different, and the approach parents took in those days was much harsher than is the case now. Whole books have been written on this topic, but this is enough to set the stage for my story.

Although we were fortunate enough to have a TV in our house growing up, like most young boys, it was a dream of mine to have my own TV so that I would not be held captive by my parents' viewing choices. Just because your father always wanted to watch the John Wayne movie did not mean that you did!

In the sixties, the family would usually gather around the single TV that each home had and watch programs together. Similar to the commonplace older tradition of sitting down to family dinners each night, this shared TV experience created a certain bonding and togetherness that no longer seems to exist in America.

In our area, we had channels two, four, five, seven, nine, eleven, thirteen, and in some cases if you could get the tuning right, channels twenty-eight and fifty-two. Channel fifty-two was of particular importance, because they showed *The Little Rascals* and *The Three Stooges.*

There was no satellite TV with 500 channels, cablevision, Netflix, Internet, or flat screens, only what you could pull in on the "rabbit ears" antenna affixed to the top of the set. Very advanced homes of the time had an antenna on top of the roof. Moreover, most people were watching TV on black-and-white sets. And no, there was no remote control. You had to get up from the couch, go over to the TV set, and manually change the channel.

As the sixties merged into the seventies, color television arrived on screen, and my hope to have my own black-and-white TV evolved into my dream to have my own color TV. People usually shopped at that time in big department stores like Sears and Roebuck. As I began to investigate the possibilities, I learned that Sears had a very nice nineteen-inch portable color TV for sale for the princely sum of $300. In the usual calculating way of children who have no real power except for their ability to influence their parents, I concocted a plan of attack.

My mother and father conferred about this as a possible Christmas present. I was not privy to the conversation, but I assume it was not a very smooth one, as they were not on the best of terms after their contentious divorce some years prior. In any event, my father sent my mother a check and the TV became my present—a very nice Christmas indeed.

It is here where the story should end with me describing my many years of viewing enjoyment. As fate would have it, my new present had not gone unnoticed by my brother, who by this time had fallen into his "traveling the country" phase of life. It is a bit odd growing up with no father present in the house and a brother in the picture who is fifteen years older than you. We were not on equal footing, and he tended to take a rather stern approach when interacting with me, consistent with an image of authority.

An example of what I mean occurred one day after my mother had told me we were going over to her friend Sue's house for the evening. This was a happy event for me, as I loved Sue and enjoyed playing with her son, Stephen, who was my age. My mom told me to take a shower and get ready, and we would go.

During this period, although my brother did not live with us, he would appear unannounced at various times. As I was taking my shower, I was evidently making some noise singing some silly song, as kids tend to do when they're happy. Without warning, the shower door opened and I heard my brother yell, "*Hey!*" in a very loud and harsh voice.

He had made one of his surprise appearances and evidently took offense at my childhood version of *My Way* being butchered in the shower. After being chastised in this manner, my shower serenade ended prematurely. I should note this instance occurred before I received my new TV.

A short time after the arrival of the TV, there was another encounter in the shower, but one that was quite different in tone. Again, I'm in the shower, and again, my brother makes one of his surprise appearances. However, when he enters the bathroom this time I hear him say, "AJ?" in the softest voice you could imagine.

"AJ" was his childhood nickname for me, taking the initials of my first and middle name. Even as a very young boy I immediately knew something was up, as this was in no way consistent with his typical manner with me at that time.

Now I know what you're thinking. Didn't this bathroom have locks? This answer was yes, but the lock was a slide bolt…on the outside. That's right, you could lock the bathroom from the outside, but not from the inside. I wish I could tell you the origin of why it was this way, but I simply don't know. It does give you some insight into the type of home I grew up in.

When I answered Bubba's call to me, the shower door opened. He explained to me that he would be going on a long road trip and would like the honor of borrowing my new TV. Of course, there could be no better place to have such a conversation about this than when I was taking a shower. Due to my tender age, I didn't really feel I had the ability to reject this great "opportunity" to have my TV borrowed, so I quietly said okay. The shower door closed, and my brother was off on his next adventure with my TV in tow.

You might think, from earlier descriptions of my brother, that would be the last I ever saw of my TV, but you would be wrong. Not only did I see the TV again, but I also watched it many times, but not in the way you might assume.

After many months with no sign of my TV being returned, it was time for my summer trip to see my father in Georgia. As incredible as it may seem, my brother was living with his girlfriend in an apartment close to where my father lived. I don't really know how that happened, but I believed this would be my last chance to reacquire my TV. I pestered my father about this, telling him we should go over and claim my TV, reminding him that it was his money that paid for it and he was not getting the proper value, so to speak.

He agreed, and off we went to see my brother about getting my TV. There was a very long discussion between my brother and my father about the TV, but ultimately my brother agreed to return it. We loaded it into the car and drove back to the house in Tucker. Now it was simply a matter of shipping it back to my home in the Los Angeles area. We were practically home free.

My father had a console TV in the family room of his house, but no TV in the bedroom. Since it was going to be several weeks before I returned to Los Angeles, he suggested we place it in the bedroom and watch it there until I finished my visit. That sounded good to me, and he placed it on top of a long dresser in his bedroom. We did watch it quite a bit in there until I left. Every summer when I returned to see my father, we watched it again, until many years later when it finally gave out.

Yes, you understood it correctly. Once that TV was put on the dresser, it never moved again until it was sent to the dump. Oh sure, there was much talk of sending it back, but once my father and stepmother got accustomed to watching color TV in their bedroom, the fate of that TV was sealed. A replacement set, you might ask? No such luck. Thus, George and Bubba, for one of the few times in their lives, had collaborated effectively to deprive me of my Christmas present. I don't think either lost too much sleep about it.

Don't feel too bad for me. I've recovered quite nicely. I have multiple, large flat-screen TVs in my home now, with access to every channel in the universe. Oh, and this time they're bolted to the wall. The real gift my brother and father gave me, without intending to do so, was that I now probably have more appreciation for watching my own color TV than most anyone else ever could. I think that has to count for something.

A short postscript: many years after this incident took place, I asked my brother if he remembered ever borrowing a TV from me when I was a little boy. He said no. I guess there are reasons why I remember it so vividly and he does not remember it at all.

20

THE GUN

My favorite picture with my father.

My father, George, was never much of a collector of guns. He was not a hunter and as such didn't possess any hunting rifles. Nor did he ever have any professional need for such weapons. However, he did have a small revolver, which he kept in his bottom desk drawer. Over the years he would take it out and show it to me with much pride. He told me that he kept it for personal protection so that he could "take care of business" if he needed to. I would have never guessed that one day I would become the business he needed to take care of.

The story really starts in an odd way, with my first pair of contact lenses at the age of sixteen on my annual Tucker trip. Back in those days, you could get soft or hard contact lenses. The soft ones felt much better in your eye right from the start. The advantage of the hard ones was that the visual acuity was a little better and they were cheaper. The disadvantage was that it took a couple of weeks for your eyes to get used to having this hard foreign object resting on your eyeballs, and during that time you were miserably uncomfortable.

I had worn glasses since the fourth grade and was used to them. However, with becoming more active in sports, it made more sense to experiment with the contacts. Further, the tender vanity that is in place at such a time in life made the contacts quite appealing to a young boy transitioning into a man.

A decision was made to go with the hard contact lenses, which I began wearing each day, gradually increasing the amount of wear time. I did not take well to these. I don't know if I struggled more than most, but I just didn't seem to be acclimating well to the lenses, and the constant discomfort no doubt had an effect on my mood and demeanor. Ultimately I abandoned the hard lenses for the soft ones, which I still wear on occasion to this day. However, I wanted to do my best to give them a fair trial, so I continued to bite the bullet hoping they would become more comfortable as time wore on.

About a week into the process, with the hard contact lenses in my eyes, George's wife Pauline arrived home with a batch of groceries. As was the custom, George and I went out to the carport to collect the groceries from the trunk of the car. It just so happened that I was the one who grabbed the last bag, and so it fell to me to close the trunk. I slammed it down, not really hard, but not lightly either. The sole reason was because of the pain and discomfort I was experiencing in my eyes. My father had gotten to the door of the house when I did this, and he continued inside with his bags of groceries.

I made my way to the door leading into the house. I opened it and went inside. I made a left turn, which would take me into the front room area that you walked through in order to get to the kitchen. Before I made it into the kitchen, I was confronted by George, who had retrieved his gun from the office and was pointing it at me. I stood about seven feet away from him with the groceries in my arms. Pauline was standing in the room with us, not making a move or a sound.

He went into a very long rant where he listed his heretofore unmentioned grievances against me. I can't remember all of what he said, first because it was such an unexpected event and second because I was carefully evaluating my limited options. I didn't really understand what was happening. There were no prior arguments or confrontations that had occurred during my visit. He had not until that point expressed any particular displeasure toward me, nor had I expressed any complaints, except for the strong discomfort I was experiencing with my eyes.

At some point, pretty long into his ravings, it dawned on me he was upset because I had slammed the trunk. As he continued on it also became clear that he had a theory as to why I had slammed it. I say theory, but it really was an unassailable conclusion he had come to. He was convinced the reason I had slammed the trunk was as an expression of my displeasure with being expected to come out and help bring in the groceries. This despite the fact that I had brought in the groceries before on countless occasions over the years without complaining or slamming the trunk.

As I considered my options, I concluded there were three ways to go: 1) Continue into the kitchen with the groceries, and then make a run for it out the back door, 2) Slowly close the distance between us and make a move for the gun, and 3) Hold my ground and hope that he would eventually run out of steam before he pulled the trigger.

I chose option three, to hold my ground. A secondary decision of this option was whether I should engage in a dialogue with him. He really wasn't asking me any questions. He was just raving away about the grievances he had that he felt were exemplified by my action of slamming the trunk. However, it crossed my mind that if I could convince him that yes, I did slam the trunk, but it was not for the reason he believed, that might defuse him.

After mulling this over quite a bit, I chose against it. My reason was that I didn't think he would believe me in the heat of the moment. I thought he would simply think this was more of my trickery to try and get out of the responsibility of my actions and that it would enrage him that much more.

There's an old saying that you can't argue with results, and in this case, I got the desired result with option three. He did finally burn himself out, but it took quite a while for him to do so. There is also an old saying that you can't argue with a shotgun. I would add that you can't argue with a snub-nose .38 either.

Estimating time in that kind of situation is very difficult, but my best guess is that it took him around five minutes to exhaust himself, all the while waving the gun around and pointing it in my direction. He finally turned around and went back to his office. I made eye contact with Pauline, who had also evidently gone with option three. She neither did nor said anything during the entire encounter.

Although I certainly could have, I did not call the local authorities. I have zero doubt that he would have denied his actions, and Pauline would have "corroborated" his version. I also have no doubt that had he actually shot me, they would have covered it up by claiming that I committed suicide right after I brought in the groceries! Forensics in a small town in the sixties were not too advanced, so in all likelihood, he would have gotten away with it. I decided that I should cut my trip short and head home, and that is exactly what I did.

I have told this story to many people over the years, so I know what the typical questions are. The first one, particularly from people who know my father's reputation, was if he was drunk or had been drinking. They are looking to place some of the blame on the blurred judgment that results from alcohol. The answer is that he was not drinking; he was fully sober that day.

People ask if he had ever displayed this type of violent behavior toward me before. The answer to that one is also no. He had never struck me before or tried to abuse me physically, much less pull a gun on me. Again, it is normal to think that perhaps this was part of an escalating pattern that culminated in this incident, but that is not the case either.

Another common thought is that perhaps the gun was unloaded. I can't say with certainty whether the gun was loaded. I can only say that every single time he showed it to me in his office, it was loaded.

People ask if I thought there was a real possibility of him actually shooting me. Again, I can't say for sure if he was actively considering this no matter my reactions to him, or if perhaps I reacted in the "right" way with silence and deference, so he therefore made the decision not to shoot. Could it have all been a big bluff? Well, that's always possible. All I can say is that with the look in his eye, the way he was behaving, and the fact that his judgment gears had clearly been stripped, the most plausible theory is that actually shooting me was at least an outside possibility.

The area of most intrigue for people in this story is how a man could threaten to shoot and perhaps kill his 16-year-old son over slamming a car trunk. Isn't a trunk designed to be slammed? Moreover, even if his son slammed the trunk, and even if it was for the reason he mistakenly believed, how would that possibly warrant getting a gun to settle the score? This simply does not compute in any way, shape, or form for people, and I understand their reaction because I feel the same way.

I've had many years to think over this incident, and the bottom line is that I will never know all the particulars of his thinking or intentions. This is not a situation I ever discussed with my father after the fact, and even if I did, I certainly don't think he could explain his actions in any way that made sense. He never brought it up to me again, and he never apologized or said he was out of line.

All that said, I'm going to give you my best shot at what was really going on. I believe this incident wasn't really about the slamming of the trunk or the purported rage at me taking this action to demonstrate my displeasure at having to bring in the groceries. I think it was really about an insecure man who had been looking for an opportunity to assert himself as the "alpha" male of the house.

This was the first time since he moved to Tucker that there was another man living in the house, albeit a very young one. It may also be that Pauline made some innocuous remark about my striking physical transformation, and he had decided to show her who the "real" man of the house was.

At the time of the incident I was 16 years old, going on seventeen. I was about 5' 10", and 200 pounds, already quite a bit larger than my father. Further, as a very active athlete in football, tennis, and putting the shot in track and field, I had an athlete's body, something my father never possessed even in his youth. I had been weightlifting seriously for almost five years, and my body had developed as a result in a way that was strong and muscular. I was doing well in school and appeared to be headed toward college, something my father had never done. I was rapidly transitioning from the boy he had always known into a powerful man.

I had skipped the previous year's trip to Tucker for a variety of reasons, so he had not seen me in two years and the change was great. In the final analysis, I believe instead of my father taking pride in the way I was progressing into a man, he felt threatened. This may not have even been in a conscious way. My thought is that as my visit continued, he looked for a way to make a statement and he found the rationale for his actions in my slamming of the trunk. Of course, if accurate, this is disgraceful, but the truth of the matter is that his behavior was disgraceful even if I am wrong in my analysis.

Perhaps further supporting this alpha male theory is that Pauline was present to see the whole show. Could this have been a coincidence? Maybe, but my instincts tell me that he chose the confrontation location based on the fact she was present. It is also interesting to note that he did not physically confront me, challenge me to a fight, or even take a swing at me. You would think that would be the logical thing to do if you were so enraged that you felt violence was the answer. My guess is that he discarded those notions based on not liking the odds.

I've never had my ass kicked by an accountant either before or after this incident, and I think he may have determined that it wasn't going to occur that time either. Instead, he went right to the firearm approach, thus putting the odds of a successful confrontation in front of his beloved greatly in his favor. To get beaten to a pulp by your young son in your home in front of your wife after you had been the one to start the fight would have perhaps been too much humiliation to risk.

In the end, I can't prove my theory of why this situation occurred. I can only say that I knew my father, I was present when this occurred, and I'm sure I've spent more time going over what occurred in my mind than anyone else. As such, this is my best take on what motivated his actions. Not one of my favorite stories, but I lived to tell the tale. Sometimes that's the best you can hope for. You can't really explain the inexplicable.

21

BALDWIN

Little League.

I was blessed to go to the same elementary school in Alhambra, California from kindergarten through eighth-grade. It was called Martha

Baldwin Elementary, and for the most part I went through all nine years there with the same kids. These are the kinds of friendships and relationships that tend to stand the test of time, at least as far as one's memory is concerned.

My first remembrance of the possibility of school goes back to when my mom drove up to a local preschool and took the name and information off of the sign, to inquire about me attending. I'm not really sure what motivated me to say this, because I really didn't know much about school, be it this one or any other. However, I said, "I'm not going there." I don't know if it was because of my assertion or other factors at play, but I did not go there or anywhere else until I started kindergarten.

I have quite a few memories of kindergarten, including the start. They kept us busy with a variety of activities throughout our first day. I had no idea how to know when the day would end, and I really didn't think much about it. However, there was a wall of windows, and I noticed at one point that my mom had arrived and was parked on the street. I got up and headed for the door, and they asked me where I was going. I told them I was going to leave, as my mom was here to pick me up.

This was my first information about school ending at a certain time, rather than when your mom arrived. I guess I thought of it the same way as when I was at a friend's house. You didn't leave when a certain time came, you left when your mom came to get you. This was the first moment for me where I learned about the clock running your life, rather than doing whatever you wanted to do.

One of our activities was making things out of clay, which would then be fired in the kiln to preserve them for their rightful posterity. I was not particularly artistic then, and not much has changed in the ensuing fifty years. However, I specifically remember making a beautiful "carrot," which I had rolled out very carefully with the clay. When the teacher came around to collect our masterpieces for the oven, she refused to collect mine. It's interesting how I still remember this transgression so many years later. Nowadays parents would file a grievance and alert the media if their child's self-esteem was affected like that.

My father had already flown the coup for Georgia by the time I went to kindergarten, and I was exchanging letters with him with my mom's help. Since I couldn't really read or write too well at that time, I'm sure my letters to him were quite interesting to read, probably filled with words like "bastard," and my mom's perennial favorite, "son of a bitch."

I remember my father's letters back to me ending with something like, "Well, I guess it's time to close now." When we wrote stories in class, helped by our teacher, each child would dutifully finish with "The End." Not me. I ended my story with, "Well, I guess it's time to close now." I remember the look on the teacher's face, which I can best describe as communicating something like, "This kid's whacked."

Whacked or not, I was able to matriculate into the first grade and beyond. One of my favorite stories of that time is the "numa-numa" kid. He was a nice boy, but he had this odd habit of saying "numa-numa" whenever things didn't go his way. He would start out slow and quiet with his numa-numas, but if things continued in a way he did not like, he would get louder and faster with the numa-numas, at which point he would begin jumping up and down.

This would end with somewhat of a crescendo of numa-numas, shouted at the top of his lungs as fast as he could get them out, while continuing to jump up and down. So, something like this: numa-numa-numa-numa-numa-numa-NUMA-NUMA-NUMA-NUMA. This would go on for the longest time, until he would finally collapse on the ground of exhaustion.

I was not alone in thinking this was the most entertaining thing I had ever seen. As such, it would cause us to do an array of things, all of which we knew would set him off. You could immediately stop the numa-numas at any time simply by giving him what he wanted. For example, if you took his toy away from him, he would start up, but if you gave it back, he would stop.

For some reason, loud music would set him off, so if you turned up a radio full blast, he would go into his routine. By moving the volume control from loud to soft and back again, you could control him like a marionette. Let's be clear, I certainly wouldn't do something like that, I'm only describing what other kids did.

I was once sitting next to another student who had a ruler. I didn't have one at that moment, but I needed one. I've never been a thief, but when he got up to go to another part of the room, I took the ruler. I anticipated he would accuse me of stealing the ruler when he returned, so

I wrote my initials on the back of it. Sure enough, he returned and said, "That's my ruler." I calmly replied, "Yeah, that's why my initials are on it," as I showed him "AH" on the back of the ruler. I gave him the ruler back when I was done. I was just messing with him.

In third grade, I bashed a girl's face in with a stick, but it's not what you think. We had a piñata day and several of the other kids had failed in their attempts to separate the candy from the donkey. I was then blindfolded, given a stick, and spun around. The kids were screaming, as kids do, and I swung hard and connected.

Unfortunately, it was Mary's face I connected with, but I only learned that later. The crowd got deathly quiet and the blindfold was removed from me. I had no idea what had happened. Eventually we trudged back to the room, and I overheard two other kids talking about how Mary's parents might sue my parents. I endured the harsh stares from teachers and other kids, but still had no idea what had happened. Obviously, though, I was the bad guy.

The teacher placed a small amount of candy on everyone's desk, including mine. She talked in somber tones about what a bad thing had happened. I eventually pieced it together, but then, as now, I still don't understand how it was my fault. A young child is blindfolded, intentionally disoriented, given a stick and told to swing away, all the while not being properly guided and supervised. I learned something important that day: that sometimes you get the blame and those who should take the blame fail to step up. I'm sorry Mary; I didn't mean to.

In fifth grade, I was sitting at my desk when my friend Joey passed by. He had not learned his lesson to give me a wide berth, and so he got a punch in the butt for his trouble when he went by my "sphere of influence." All in good fun. Boys will be boys. However, when Joey turned to face me after his transgression had been addressed, I noticed his face had changed into Cynthia's, a very nice girl who was innocently walking by my desk. How I mistook her butt for Joey's, I'll never know, but I must have turned several shades of red as I apologized to her.

Once I moved on to junior high, when I was much more mature, I came into French class and noticed my friend Mark sitting there. We had those kinds of desks where the chair and the table were attached. As I got to the desk behind Mark, I thought I'd give him a little "good morning" by lowering the desk slightly, so it would line up in between the slats, where it would be propelled right into Mark's back. All in good fun. Boys will be boys.

However, when Mark turned around to face me, I noticed that his face had changed into Susan's, a nice young girl who had made the mistake of temporarily sitting at Mark's desk to talk to someone before class. I went through my now normal protocol of several shades of red followed by apologies. Some people never learn, and in this case, that someone was me.

There is always one kid in school who is the "whipping boy," and in our group it was Jeff, who makes guest appearances in other chapters as well. Jeff was always in trouble, including when he didn't get the 3-D baseball card he sent away for as part of a breakfast cereal promotion. Most of us would let it go, but not Jeff. He wrote a letter to the cereal headquarters in Battle Creek, Michigan, stating that it was his intention to firebomb their offices. I don't know what came of this, but I'm sure today they would call the FBI.

Jeff was the kind of guy who would put a coin in a newspaper vending machine and then take all the papers. This would also apply to the pornographic newspapers, which he loved to collect in bulk. One of his favorite pastimes was going to the "wash," which was a flood control channel where typically a small amount of water would flow. He would stand on the bridge and drop off pages of the porn newspapers into the flowing water. His goal was for it to land in the water with the most graphic pictures face up.

He believed that if he accomplished this, that there would be old ladies downstream who, when crossing the bridges, would see these pictures and be appalled. I doubt this ever happened, but I think for Jeff it happened in his mind and that was all that mattered to him.

Another classic Jeff incident occurred during halftime of a league basketball game in eighth grade. We were huddled in an alcove of a gymnasium with our coach giving us instructions on how we should play in the second half. As it happens, Jeff was near the opening of the alcove when a young woman stuck her head inside. Jeff, in his inimitable way, said, "Hey Tits, get out of here!" As we were to learn momentarily, the woman was our coach's wife. To say that Jeff had no impulse control would be an understatement. He could not stop himself from saying what popped into his head.

Such outbursts occurred even in his own family. Although I was not present at this event, I heard it from several reliable sources who were there. Jeff was having his birthday party with a bunch of kids in the backyard. Jeff had been instructed by his father to go inside and get some more drinks. As he exited the backdoor, his father told him to hurry up with those drinks. Jeff said to him, "I am, you son of a bitch." This caused his father to go over to him and slap him in the face in front of all the kids. Now Jeff knew his father and knew his father's likely reaction, but again, he couldn't help himself.

Another of Jeff's specialties was taking those tear-off cards from magazines and signing his classmates up for magazine subscriptions, which would then begin arriving at their homes followed later by a bill. I know you must be thinking about all those phony subscriptions that kids got for *Sports Illustrated* and *People Magazine.* Alas, this was not how Jeff did things. The magazines that would begin to arrive addressed to his classmates were *Playboy*® and *Penthouse*®.

In those days, most of the mothers stayed at home while the fathers worked, thus, in almost all cases, it was Mom who first got to see her son's newfound taste in magazines. This did not sit well with the moms of the time and punishment was imposed immediately. The utterly laughable pleas by their boys that they did not sign up for any such subscriptions were summarily dismissed as lacking in credibility. Jeff never got to see any of this play out in person, but I think he took just as much enjoyment imagining how it played out in his own mind.

As I moved through the grades at Martha Baldwin, my interests moved to those of the female persuasion. Typically the way it works is that you have an infatuation with one girl, then about twenty minutes later a different one, and so on. Not me. For me it was Joan, and this stood the test of time from about second grade all the way through eighth grade.

Sadly for me, this was an unrequited relationship, but at least she was never mean to me as my tongue convulsed while I tried to talk to her. I'd like to say that as the grades progressed I got progressively smoother in my interactions with Joan, but I just don't believe this was the case. After eighth grade graduation, I never saw her again, but she will be forever fixed in my mind.

One who really stands out to me is Cindy, who was the only girl I can remember who treated me with genuine kindness and warmth during these times. To say this stood out would be an understatement. I fit in well with the boys, but with the girls, it was a lost cause. Cindy was the exception, and I'll always be grateful to her for her sweetness and kindness. I'll let you in on a little secret. Cindy and I are still friends to this day.

As I got older, I was heavily involved in sports, including Little League. I remember Woody Allen once talking about being involved in the Boys Club when he was a kid, where he had the opportunity to be abused by boys of "all creeds and colors." My skillset in baseball was such that I was typically playing with boys who were much older, so I can relate a bit to what he said. I gave as good as I got, older boys or not.

I was in Cub Scouts for a while, too, which I enjoyed. I would wear my little uniform to class on the days we would meet after school, and a bigger shot you've never seen. In our "den" was my friend Steve, who ended up becoming the mayor of the town. We would play endless games of football, basketball, and ping pong at his house.

Our football games were typically played in the street due to yard-size limitations. The street was not heavily traveled, so it was only occasionally we would get interrupted. However, on one particular day it kept happening, and I had had it. When the next car came on the street, I didn't move right away and gave the driver a pretty good Clint Eastwood-type stare down. As I slowly strolled out of the street in full command of the situation, I continued my drop-dead stare at the driver as she passed. She then said hello to me. It was Mrs. Baker, the principal of the school. Who else would it have been?

Basketball was a game we loved to play, and we played it hard, so much so that we began referring to it as "casketball." Meaning, no casket, no foul. The influx of Asian students into the community was just beginning at that time, and one of the boys who joined our class was named Dick.

In typical young boy fashion, he was immediately christened as "Prick," and it stuck. I'm not sure how this change from one name to another was warranted considering his actual name, but such decisions were not run by the campus academic committee beforehand. He didn't seem to mind, and although he was not athletically gifted, he was a "gamer" in that he would go out there and give it all he had, even though the rules of basketball seemed a bit of a mystery to him, as was the case with the English language.

One thing he did learn quickly was the concept of a foul. There were no referees on the playground, so everyone called their own fouls. Dick became quite enamored of this concept and called fouls on a pretty regular basis. Normally this would not have been tolerated, and you would get a smack for calling too many fouls; however, with Dick it was allowed because it was so funny.

Whenever Dick felt that he had been inappropriately roughed up as he handled the basketball, he would scream at the top of his lungs, "Foul!" There were two aspects about this that we found humorous. First, he really didn't say "foul," it came out more like "faw." For some reason we found this very funny, but what was even better was the extraordinary indignation that came across in his voice when he said it. The combination of these two things would have us laughing loudly.

Although we let Dick have his fouls, like a lot of things, there was an unintended consequence in that we would foul him mercilessly just to hear him say it. No matter how many times we fouled him, his passion for calling the foul, and his accompanying indignation, was undiminished. I can still hear him say it to this day, and it makes me chuckle almost forty-five years later.

I played and was good at most all sports. One of the big deals at that school was the student/faculty games that were played each year. The faculty would play against the eighth grade students, typically in basketball and softball. As a kid, I watched this every year along with the whole school, and every year the eighth graders lost. Our group couldn't wait to get our turn when we became eighth graders. We played the basketball game first, which resulted in a 14-14 tie. How this tie was allowed to stand, I'll never know. I had a good game: eight points of those fourteen were mine.

We won the softball game 8-4 against the faculty. I was two-for-two, with two singles, two walks, and four runs scored. I don't know whether the faculty returned to dominance in the ensuing years, but I know we did our job. I will always remember that fondly. I was the first baseman that day, so I caught the ball for the last out of the game. My only regret is that I should have kept that ball and had it signed by all the players.

Mr. Chavez was the "cool" teacher of the school. He started a bowling league, which was great fun. Once a week, we were allowed to get out of school early and go down to the bowling alley to play in a league we had formed. He also started a tennis program. Every year there would be a tennis tournament for eighth graders. It was my goal to be the tennis champion of the school, and that's what happened. I received a nice trophy at a school assembly for that, and it is a very fond memory.

I was always a physical and rambunctious kid. I did not look to start fights, but I certainly didn't back down from them either. There was a kid named Ryan, who I actually got along with pretty well; he was a notorious fighter and was always up in the school office receiving some sort of discipline. One day we got into it on the playground, and he stormed off. In my strategic mode, knowing Ryan very well, my guess was that he would head off to the bike cages and let the air out of my tires.

I went over to the bike area, and that was exactly what he was doing. I came up behind him and drove some very hard blows into his ribs from both sides. My favorite boxer at the time was Joe Frazier, and I did my best impersonation of "Smokin' Joe's" blistering body shots. I don't think Ryan was as much of a fan of Joe Frazier as I was after I got through with him. He again stormed off, this time saying he was going to go up to the office and lodge a complaint.

I don't know if they laughed in Ryan's face or not, but I'm sure they did laugh at this guy complaining about getting beaten by another kid. For many years it had been other kids coming up to the office to complain about him. Two interesting things occurred as a result of this. First, they never even bothered to call me up to the office. Second, my teacher, who had evidently gotten wind of this in the faculty lounge came up to me as the bell rang. She leaned down until she was eye-to-eye with me and said, "Did you beat up Ryan?" I said yes, and she said, "Good for you."

I got off one of my best lines on this teacher. She was instructing us in math, and the class was not performing well. As her frustration grew, she finally said, "What are you going to tell them when you get to high school?"

Without missing a beat, I shouted, "We'll tell them you didn't teach us." That brought the house down, and the look on her face was priceless. I must tell you, I thought I saw just a trace of a smile on her face.

One of the coolest things I've ever done was to organize a thirty-year reunion for my eighth grade graduating class. I went to high school in another city, so I did not have the opportunity to continue on in school with any of these people, which I was quite disturbed about. I've never been an organizer-type, but for some reason, I just decided one day I was going to do it.

We had a great turnout, and it was far more fun than any of the high school reunions I've attended. Further, the number of success stories out of that little graduating class was amazing. In addition to our esteemed mayor, there were multiple physicians, a dentist, several successful businessmen, a firefighter, a world-class automobile designer, and many others who have done quite well. It was a night to remember, and I will place it into the photo book in my mind of my great time at Martha Baldwin.

22

RUNNING THE RACE

On the lawnmower, with Cathy the Maid.

"There's nothing that smells worse than a wet nigger." The comment was made by my father with no detectable anger or animation. It was said in the same way someone might remark about a change in the weather. We were traveling on the freeway after a summer rainstorm had hit and were coming up on an old pick-up truck with a number of black men in the bed. The front windows of our car were cracked open, as was the custom in that vehicle. The men had been caught in the pick-up truck during the storm, and they were soaked.

As we passed the truck and the remark was made, there was no visible reaction on the part of my father's wife Pauline. My sense at the time was that she was in agreement, but that the assertion was so indisputable it was hardly worthy of a verbal response. That was just my impression as a child at the time, but looking back on it I think it's accurate. I wasn't sure why black men would smell worse than any other color, but they seemed to take it as an accepted fact. Had I questioned it, my best guess is I would have been laughed at for childish ignorance.

Racial stereotypes were not confined merely to African-Americans. The Atlanta Braves baseball team had a mascot at the time known as "Chief Noc-A-Homa." As you might gather from his name, he was quite fond of having the Braves' players hit home runs. He resided in a tepee just beyond the outfield fence, and he engaged in various activities during the game.

One of my favorite of these was when he would send smoke signals to the players. Other than letting them know they should hit a home run, I'm not sure what he may have been communicating, but as a little boy, it was fascinating to watch.

The big event though was when someone from the home team did knock one over the fence. The Chief would dance and celebrate like a madman, with us doing so right along with him. If his job was to get the home fans fired up, he was successful at that without a doubt.

Today such a mascot as this would be met with a frown at a minimum, and probably even protests. However, at the time, we didn't think a thing about it. The Chief was simply part of the home team, and we rooted together for the Braves to win.

As modern sensibilities took hold, the Chief was quietly removed from his post. However, he lives on in perpetuity with an entry in Wikipedia, a recorded throwback to a different time.

A more malignant form of racism on display during those times was a man named JB Stoner, who was a candidate for governor in Georgia in that era. JB was a proud white supremacist who was often on TV in political ads in his run for governor. In the ads, he described his vision for the state were he to be elected governor, and let's just say kind treatment toward blacks was not part of his platform.

I don't remember all of what was said in his commercials, but one part remains very clear in my mind. He assured us that as governor he would put a stop to the niggers "messing with our white women." Now, as a child, I wasn't really sure what qualified as messing with our white women, but I knew it wasn't good in JB's view. I must say he was convincing, in that if you wanted this kind of messing around to be stopped, JB was the guy to do it.

In today's society what I'm describing is utterly unthinkable, and it may be that some younger people are skeptical that such a thing could have occurred. However, if you go on YouTube, there are some video clips of JB that will provide corroborative evidence of what I'm saying, including a rollicking debate with talk show host Wally George.

As a general rule, I believe my father did not dislike black people, as long as they "knew their place." What place was this? I venture to say lower on the pecking order than whites, deferential to whites, and typically in the service of whites. Any black person meeting this criteria was treated with kindness and respect by my father.

An example of this was Leon the "yard boogie." Yes, that is really what he referred to him as, at least to us. My father's property was a few acres, and throughout most of his life he mowed it himself on a riding lawn mower. There was a time, though, when he employed Leon to do the work. I observed that my father seemed to like him, and their interactions were very friendly. I also had the impression that he paid Leon very well.

Then there were the "house boogies." These were two women who would come in on occasion and clean the house. They didn't drive, or perhaps didn't have access to a car, so we had to pick them up. I still remember it to this day. We drove our Cadillac into the worst housing area I've ever seen before or since.

To say we stood out like a sore thumb in that neighborhood in our Cadillac would be an understatement, but my father and his wife didn't seem to give it a second thought. We picked up the two women and brought them back to the house, where they did the cleaning. Late in the day, we returned them to whence they came.

Again, these ladies were treated with respect, and they seemed to have a comfortable and practiced rapport with my dad. As with Leon, I believe they were happy to get the work, and I think he compensated them very well. I don't remember their names, but they, along with Leon, were examples of relationships my father had with black people during that time. He did not hate these people, and actually seemed to enjoy having them around. However, they met the above criteria about knowing their place.

For a period of time we also had a live-in maid named Cathy. She was an older white woman with short, grey hair combed exactly as you might expect in a man of that era. She was a very opinionated person, who could tell you how things should be in all facets of domestic and foreign policy. To me, the most unique thing about Cathy was that I can never recall her doing any housework. Not once. I'm sure she must have, but during my month on the premises, I didn't see it.

My favorite story about Cathy involves her going up on the roof. I'm not really sure why she found going up on the roof so appealing, but if I were to venture a guess, it would be that no one could see her. This would facilitate not working quite well. Having a radio and the newspaper up on the roof might be a nice way to kill a couple of hours, especially when the alternative was working. The purported reason for her going up top was to clean off the tree leaves from the roof and the gutters, but I don't think this was her primary objective. When she advised George and Pauline where she had been going, they specifically told her not to go up there again.

It may not shock you to learn that Cathy did not follow orders very well, and the result was a nasty fall from the roof that resulted in multiple broken bones. Although I would have never wished for this to happen to Cathy, even as insubordinate as she was, I must admit it led to one of the more amusing situations to have ever happened in the Tucker house.

For a number of months after her fall, Cathy was on bedrest at the house, waited on hand-and-foot by George and Pauline. Had there been "pay per view" events at the time, no doubt this would have been shown. The idea of them, in essence, acting as Cathy's servant still brings a smile to my face. When I talk to anyone who was in the know about that situation, like my brother or my friend Dale, one of us will invariably say,

"Remember when the maid fell off the roof?" Just that sentence alone can bring laughter to us.

When Cathy was finally back in "top form," George decided they didn't need a live-in maid anymore, but I have no doubt that he paid her quite a bit of money to leave quietly. The nice black ladies magically reappeared to take care of the housekeeping needs. I'm not sure if he would have ever asked one of them to become a live-in maid had the situation with Cathy never occurred. What I do know for sure is that no person, black or white, ever came to serve again as a live-in maid. I think one Cathy was enough to last them a lifetime.

23

PLAYBOY® AND ME

I finally made it to The Mansion, and met The Man.

As was the case with most young boys back in the sixties, I had a fascination with *Playboy® Magazine.* Now I know what you're thinking, and you are right, but there was more to it than that. The girls were great, but I really did read the articles, even back then. Further, I was interested in this "Playboy® Philosophy" that seemed to be a way to a sophisticated and fanciful lifestyle. Although I wasn't trying to bypass my growing-up phase, I was looking to achieve that sophistication at a more accelerated rate than my current course at that time would dictate.

My first exposure to such things was pretty typical. My classmate, Jeff, who you are acquainted with from prior chapters, had brought the magazine to school after, no doubt, bagging it from the local liquor store when the clerk was distracted. Although you may not know Jeff, you know the kind of guy—troublemaker, mouthy, always doing what he was told not to do. However, in this instance, he was providing an important service to young boys like me. After all, the lifetime chase had to start somewhere, didn't it?

A good example of Jeff's antics was when he flooded our classroom. Now mind you, a student flooding a classroom might not seem that unusual to you, but Jeff flooded it while class was in session. Adding further insult to injury, I got caught up in the blame for the whole mess.

It all started when I got a drink at the water fountain in the back of the room. I noticed that the fountain was loose and could be turned away from the sink it emptied into. This fountain had a strong stream of water, and it was my calculation that if I manipulated it just so, I could turn it on and hit my friend Jerry on top of the head with a squirt of water. Jerry's desk was all the way in the back of the room, close to the fountain. I know it sounds crazy, but this proved an irresistible impulse to a young man.

I turned the fountain, aimed it with military precision, and fired—direct hit. Jerry never knew what hit him, and I was delighted. Finally, I had achieved something of significance in school. It was then that I made my fatal mistake by telling Jeff that the fountain could be moved and directed to classmates in the back of the room. As was usually the case with Jeff, he took it to the next level, which was almost always not good.

While I went back to my desk, Jeff unscrewed the fountain. Round and round he went, with an ending that could only be ugly. What possessed him to continue on this mission I don't know, but he did. The next thing you knew, gusher! In what must have been a smaller version of what happens with Texas oilmen, the water was blasting straight up into the ceiling and splattering everywhere. I was in convulsions with laughter, and the best part was there was no way I could get in trouble. I had nothing to do with unscrewing the fountain. Sadly, the principal ultimately had a contrasting view on this matter.

What was already an amusing situation got even funnier as Jeff began to make a yeoman's effort to screw the fountain back on. This resembled something out of The Three Stooges. Jeff looked as if he had been sprayed with a fire hose as he continued to work with vigor, but it was no use; the water pressure was just too great. By now the class had moved toward the center of the room, and the teacher had gone into authority mode. The class was evacuated as water began to pool on the floor. The janitor was summoned, but somehow his response was less than rapid. By the time they got the water shut off, it was a bit of a class tide pool.

Well, that's definitely the maddest I've ever seen a principal. Jeff laid *me* flat out as the mastermind of the operation. My total ambition was to give Jerry a little "hello" soak from his old friend. Surely the principal, when he heard of my lack of culpability, would place all the blame where it belonged. That was not what happened, as I was not even allowed to present my case.

Jeff and I served a week of clean-up and lunch detention—my first and last time sentenced to hard labor. I was a pretty good kid, but I learned that day that the Jeffs of the world will always take it to the next level, and if you're close by, you'll go for the ride.

Still, I feel I owe Jeff for that first eye-opening experience with *Playboy*®. Subsequent to that, I was able to develop my own "collection," which came about through various methods of acquisition. One example of this was the "operation," as conceived by my friend Oliver when we were both about eight-years old.

As was often the case with Oliver, he had a unique take on things, and this included magazines with nude pictures in them. He was a fan of *Playboy*®, but he also explained to me there was another magazine of this type, one which tended to focus more on one specific part of a woman's anatomy. He told me the name of the magazine was *Penthouse*®, but that was just a code name. Although it's been over four decades since he said this, I'm going to try and quote him, because I think what he said warrants that level of respect. He said, "It's really called Pusshouse, but they can't say that."

Oliver was a creative genius. He was one of those guys you would think would end up working in animation at Disney®. On the day in question, he had spotted a *Playboy*® sitting on a table near an open window. The magazine was owned by a tenant at my house. At the time, we lived at the two-story brick house in Alhambra, California. My mom and I lived on the top floor, and we rented out the bottom floor to a man named Gary.

Oliver planned this operation as soon as he saw the target-rich environment. You might think this would be easy. We would simply pop open the screen, reach inside, take the magazine, and be on our way. However, as you would perhaps say nowadays, that was not how Oliver rolled.

Such an amateurish effort was not his style. No, his plan involved much more precision, imagination and daring. He planned to take the magazine, remove the centerfold, and replace it in the exact position he found it. I can't really explain it now, but at the time it seemed to me the work of a mastermind, and I said to count me in. So, with the tenant gone, we executed the plan.

It would be a quick matter to take the magazine, rip out the centerfold, and replace it, but again, that would qualify for amateur hour. After taking the magazine and retreating to our secret bunker, we carefully pried up the staple prongs, gently removed the centerfold and mashed the staple prongs back into place. We put the magazine back into the position on the table we had memorized, and thus another piece of treasure was added to the collection, which by now Oliver and I had pooled together.

I've often wondered about Gary and whether he ever looked at that magazine again. I know he didn't look at the centerfold again, but what I don't know is whether he had looked at it prior to our operation. If he had not looked at the magazine yet, he might have thought he got a factory defect. If, on the other hand, he knew the centerfold was there, I would pay to this day to have seen the look on his face when he discovered the centerfold had vanished. In any event, Gary never reported it to my mom, perhaps because it may have been uncomfortable for him to talk to a middle-aged woman about his missing centerfold, demanding it be restored to its rightful owner. Yes, it was the perfect crime.

I'm sure Gary had his own collection as a young boy, and no doubt he acquired said collection through less than aboveboard means. Gary, if you're reading this, I'm sorry, but I think it may just be the way things go. The circle of life, if you will, for young boys. Although you may not have been involved in accumulating your collection through such sophisticated operations, surely there was somebody somewhere whose collection got smaller as yours got larger.

Sadly, like millions of other young boys, my collection was discovered and disposed of by my mother, despite my brilliant hiding place. In my room, there was a built-in closet, below which there was a huge drawer, about five feet by two feet. No, I didn't put the collection in the drawer, I'm not an idiot. What I did do was pull out the entire drawer, which really took some doing. I placed my collection underneath the drawer area and put the drawer back.

There is absolutely no reason why someone would remove the drawer for any motivation other than to paint or to retrieve something underneath it. Since my mother had nothing stored under there, and we were not painting, it was as snug as a bug in a rug.

As was the case with Oliver, that was not the way my mom rolled. For some reason, inexplicable even by someone at the Einstein-level, my mom decided to straighten out my drawer. There was really no particular reason for her to do that, but if one was going to do it, I would imagine you would simply pull the drawer out, straighten it, and push it back in. Since it was my mom, that is not what she did. You guessed it, she pulled it all the way out and dragged it into the other room to straighten it. Thus, my collection bit the dust.

I know I'm not the first one to have had this happen, so I know there are many of you who can relate to the feeling of coming home and facing a catastrophe such as this. I've recovered, to some extent, from this trauma, but I can assure you those images still exist in the archives of my mind, and no, they're not stuck together.

I had my share of *Playboy*® experiences in Tucker as well. As Dale and I hung out in the tenant's downstairs bachelor pad at my dad's house, we would typically have his collection laid out all over the floor while the man was at work. The Manhattan Project was not handled with any more attention to detail than that in which we pored over those magazines. No detail was left unexamined, and I'm sure if we had electron microscopes those would have been pressed into service as well. We were probably about seven-years old when we first started to look through these magazines, but we took our work seriously.

I realized then there was a place called the *Playboy*® Mansion, and although I was sure they weren't too hot on letting kids in, I knew it was a place I needed to go, even if it took me many years to get there. Well, it took more than a few years, it took several decades, but I made it to the Mansion.

Even better, I was able to bring my friend Dale along as well. By then he was living in the Los Angeles area. As we made our way around the Mansion grounds, we couldn't help but think back to the two little boys in Tucker trying to get things figured out. The *Playboy*® Mansion was a long way from Tucker, both in distance and years, by the time we made it there. I know we both experienced it as one of those surreal occasions that are hard to fully grasp.

I have had the good fortune to return to the Mansion for a variety of occasions, and each time I go, I can't help but be reminded of my times in Tucker. I have even had the opportunity to meet Hugh Hefner and get a picture with him. As a little boy I wasn't too sure how he might be in person, but unlike with some celebrities I've encountered, he was even better than imagined. I guess I would describe him as humble and gracious, and for that I was grateful. It would have been a shame to tarnish my great memories of *Playboy*® and my long-lost collection.

On my desk, I have a picture of Dale and me at the Mansion juxtaposed with another picture of us as little boys in Tucker. It serves as a reminder to me that many things once thought unattainable are actually possible if you can just keep the dream alive long enough.

24

EPILOGUE

All grown up.

I've told the stories you've read in this memoir to friends and acquaintances for the better part of my life. People always seemed to enjoy the tales, and often there was much laughter as I spoke of my childhood exploits, particularly those from my days in Tucker. The most common thing said went something like this: "Hey, you should really write these stories down."

Well, it took me a while to get to the point where I could look back on my childhood with the necessary maturity and perspective to place it all into context, but I finally reached that point and this book is the result. I was the only person on the planet who could write all of these particular stories, and I wanted to try and give them a life of their own beyond my own lifetime.

When I have read memoirs, I've always appreciated learning what happened to everyone at the end. If it's a good memoir, it is natural to become interested in and to some extent care for those individuals you've spent time reading about. What follows is an update on some of the main players.

My father passed on in 1998 at the age of 68. His last years were hard ones that contained many lessons he failed to learn earlier in life. How do I know? Well, because in later years he told me, including admitting he was never really much of a father to me but that he was still very proud of how I turned out. At the end of his life, all the great sums of money he had made over the years was gone. He still owned the Tucker house, but he had long ago mortgaged away all the equity in it. He lived in that house for thirty years, and that is where he died.

Shortly after his death I received correspondence from an attorney, which included my father's last will and testament. This document indicated that he had left his only asset, the title to the house, to a friend of his. Perhaps a fitting end to the relationship I had with my father.

Pauline died several years before my dad, and he surely grieved her death. They were a very good match. My father always thought of himself as the beloved family patriarch, including with Pauline's family. Even as a child I could see they merely tolerated him for Pauline's sake.

After her death, my father got a rude awakening. Once she was gone, they wouldn't even let him see the great-grandchildren, whom he had become very fond of. Her family produced a document that gave possession of certain property to them that my father thought was to be his as part of Pauline's will. He remained convinced that the documents were forgeries and that Pauline would never have betrayed him like that.

I was of the opposite opinion, believing that is exactly what she would have done. She loved my father, but when push came to shove, she loved her own children and grandkids more. The final insult was when they went into his house when he was away and removed furniture they felt they were entitled to have, furniture that Pauline had possessed prior to their marriage.

I don't think he ever really recovered from Pauline's death and the aftermath, although he took a shot at it by marrying a Brazilian woman! That was a disaster of the first magnitude, and shortly after she obtained the proper documentation she sought to live in this country, she went on her way. Coupled with the large bills for Pauline's medical care along with my father's diminished ability to work, spending his last amount of money traveling back-and-forth to Brazil and retaining immigration attorneys pretty much sunk what remained of his assets. There really is no fool like an old fool.

My mom passed away in 1995 at the age of 68. She too struggled in later years. Although her life was comfortable, that didn't seem to equate to a happy existence. She was able to leave a nice home that was paid off to me and my brother. I was in charge of the estate, and as you might guess, it was a nightmare in terms of dealing with Bubba, who produced an eleventh-hour document in an envelope just before the disbursement of the estate funds. Of course, said document entitled him to an "extra" share of the money.

When asked why he did not produce this at an earlier time, he replied that mom had given it to him before her death and he had not gotten around to opening it until just before the estate was to be settled. It was a classic Bubba move, which was countered with a classic Andrew strategic response.

I won't bore you with the details, but I will say that we predicted that Bubba would go through his money in less than a year. We were wrong. It was actually much sooner than that. It has been said that a test of a person's character is to share an inheritance with them, and I'll vouch for that. We survived it, but just barely.

My stepfather Jim died at the age of seventy-seven, within a few weeks of me finishing the manuscript for this book. I saw him regularly in the twenty years since my mom's passing, and we had a great relationship. How he stayed with my mom over the years, I'll never know, but to my eye, he is the definition of a real man.

He remarried a wonderful woman named Laura, and they had many peaceful and comfortable years until she died a couple of years before his own death. Jim came into my life when I was about sixteen-years old, and of all the blessings that have come my way in life, that was surely one of the greatest. He was a truly great dad to me.

I provided the chapters in this book to him as I wrote them, so he was able to read the whole thing before he passed away. I am thankful he got to read about my life before he came along and joined our family, but most of all, I'm glad he was able to see in writing how much I loved him and how much he meant to me. It won't be the same without him.

Jim died on Christmas Day, something I'm sure he would not have wished to do, in keeping with his caring nature. However, my family sees it to mean he was a special man indeed to be called Home on that day. Further, Christmas from now on in our family, in addition to the normal events and traditions, will be a remembrance and celebration of Jim's life. Although my mom somehow didn't seem to appreciate him too much, I sure did.

My grandmother died in 1984 at the age of 78. She was living with us during that period, and she had a heart attack. I was home at the time and administered CPR. I was able to "save" her, but she ended up in the hospital for about a month before she died. I was grateful to have that additional time to spend with her, but those were understandably not good times for her.

She said to me many times over the years, "You won't always have your old grandmammy around." She was right, and it has been thirty-years since her death. She died the day after my birthday. It was theorized at the time that she managed to hang on so that the date of her death would not be on my birthday. I wouldn't have put it past her, that's for sure.

Dorothy's character in *The Wizard of Oz* tells the Scarecrow it will be he who she will miss most of all. Of all those who have left me, I miss her the most. If I get to heaven, I will definitely look for Grandma's Hands.

Bubba is still alive and kicking, living in the Chicago area. He seems to have a contented life, but I really wouldn't know for sure. I haven't seen him in almost twenty years. He left town after our mom died and never returned. Oh, we still talk on the phone periodically, but he has been resistant to meeting in person for reasons that he has chosen not to disclose.

Whatever his flaws may be, one of my very few regrets in life is having not seen him for two decades. I would have never believed it could be, but it's a truth I've learned to accept. I still have recurring dreams where we are together and he is going to be leaving for good. I try unsuccessfully to talk him out of it and am so upset that I am crying very hard. So much so that it often wakes me up.

I've been able to maintain my friendship with Dale over a period of almost fifty-years, but it hasn't always been easy because he's a guy who tends to move around quite a bit. He followed his love of sports into the sports broadcasting field, working for many organizations, including CNN. One of the best things that happened was when he came to Los Angeles to live and work for many years. It was great fun, and we were able to be together often during those times.

In the last decade, he has spent quite a bit of time living in the Oklahoma City area, but right about the time I finished this book, he returned to California. He is my oldest friend, and I don't see him being replaced in that position anytime in this lifetime.

As for me, I've had a wonderful life. I pursued my dream by becoming a police officer and had a wonderful 25-year career in that field, ultimately retiring as a captain. About a dozen years ago, I developed a strong second career as a college professor. Along the way, I received a doctorate from Pepperdine University, wrote a couple of well-received leadership books, and have had a generally good time of it.

I still reside with my beautiful family in the Los Angeles area, in the same house now for almost thirty years. I have just about as comfortable a life as I could have ever imagined. Now that I've completed this memoir, I have only a few little things that remain on my bucket list. Life is good.

So, what kind of parent did I end up becoming after wading through all this chaos as a child? Well, I hope a pretty good one, who avoided many of the mistakes of my own parents. However, that judgement will have to be left to my own darling daughter, who is now an adult. Who knows, maybe she will one day write her own memoir about growing up with me as her father. If and until that day arrives, though, I will leave you with a little clue about how she views me as a parent.

There was a time where a friend of hers was going to be meeting me for the first time. I asked her how she had described me to the friend. My daughter told her, "He's very serious, kind of scary, but really fun." Well, that's probably the best description of me that I've heard, especially coming from such an authoritative source. I guess as a parent that is about the best description one can hope for.

Winston Churchill said, "History will be kind to me, for I intend to write it," and that is exactly what he did. I feel a similar way. As I've written this memoir I've often thought, what if we could go back 50 years or so in time and tell the people I've written about that this little boy would, many years in the future, write a book about all of it? They would have laughed all the way from the Tucker home to the nearest Waffle House®.

Writer Tobias Wolff wrote a cutting childhood memoir called *A Boy's Life.* Afterward, his mother remarked that if she had known this would happen, she might have lived a little differently. I doubt this would be the case with my cast of characters. They did what they wanted to do, and in most instances, I was left to deal with their actions and decisions. In the long-view though, the decisions about how to tell the stories were left to me.

In the notorious movie *Mommie Dearest,* at the end, after actress Joan Crawford has died, her adopted son and daughter are sitting in the lawyer's office learning that their mom evidently didn't think much of them as the will provided literally nothing for either child. The son glumly said to the daughter Christina, who ultimately wrote the memoir upon which the movie was based, "As usual, she has the last word." Christina pauses and then says, "Does she?"

It is the writer who gets the final word. I've tried hard to recount all the instances in this memoir to the best of my ability. I never wanted some sort of inauthentic or exaggerated tale, so I wrote it exactly as I remember it. I believe the stories stand on their own as they actually happened, without any need for enhancement. Although, admittedly, what is described is filtered first through the eyes of a young boy, seasoned through many decades of memory, and then viewed anew through the perspective of a mature man. I hope you enjoyed my stories of growing up.

Actor Bryan Cranston, speaking of his memoir, said he had a childhood that he wouldn't want for others, but as a storyteller, he realized that only challenging, unfortunate experiences make good stories. I know a bit of what he speaks. However, despite some of the insanity that came my way, I had a hell of a good run as a kid. I hope this memoir reflects that.

Also By Andrew J. Harvey

The Call to Lead: How Ordinary People Become Extraordinary Leaders

Leadership: Texas Hold 'Em Style (with Raymond E. Foster)

The author may be reached through his professional website at www.thecalltolead.com

Select MSI Books

Self-Help Books

A Woman's Guide to Self-Nurturing (Romer)

Creative Aging: A Baby Boomer's Guide to Successful Living (Vassiliadis & Romer)

Divorced! Survival Techniques for Singles over Forty (Romer)

How to Get Happy and Stay That Way: Practical Techniques for Putting Joy into Your Life (Romer)

How to Live from Your Heart (Hucknall)(Book of the Year Finalist)

Living Well with Chronic Illness (Charnas)

Overcoming the Odds (C. Leaver)

Publishing for Smarties: Finding a Publisher (Ham)

Recovering from Domestic Violence, Abuse, and Stalking (Romer)

Survival of the Caregiver (Snyder)

The Rose and the Sword: How to Balance Your Feminine and Masculine Energies (Bach & Hucknall)

The Widower's Guide to a New Life (Romer)(Book of the Year Finalist)

Tips and Tools for Living Well with Chronic Illness (Charnas)

Widow: A Survival Guide for the First Year (Romer)

Inspirational and Religious Books

A Believer-in-Waiting's First Encounters with God (Mahlou)

A Guide to Bliss: Transforming Your Life through Mind Expansion (Tubali)

Christmas at the Mission: A Cat's View of Catholic Beliefs and Customs (Sula)

El Poder de lo Transpersonal (Ustman)

Everybody's Little Book of Everyday Prayers (MacGregor)

How to Argue with an Atheist (Brink)

Joshuanism (Tosto)

Living in Blue Sky Mind: Basic Buddhist Teachings for a Happy Life (Diedrichs)

Passing On: How to Prepare Ourselves for the Afterlife (Romer)

Puertas a la Eternidad (Ustman)

Surviving Cancer, Healing People: One Cat's Story (Sula)

Tale of a Mission Cat (Sula)

The Seven Wisdoms of Life: A Journey into the Chakras (Tubali)(Book of the Year Finalist)

When You're Shoved from the Right, Look to Your Left: Metaphors of Islamic Humanism (O. Imady)

Memoirs

57 Steps to Paradise: Finding Love in Midlife and Beyond (Lorenz)

Blest Atheist (Mahlou)

Forget the Goal, the Journey Counts . . . 71 Jobs Later (Stites)

From Deep Within: A Forensic and Clinical Psychologist's Journey (Lewis)

Good Blood: A Journey of Healing (Schaffer)

Healing from Incest: Intimate Conversations with My Therapist (Henderson & Emerton) (Book of the Year Finalist)

It Only Hurts When I Can't Run: One Girl's Story (Parker)

Las Historias de Mi Vida (Ustman)

Of God, Rattlesnakes, and Okra (Easterling)

Road to Damascus (E. Imady)

The Optimistic Food Addict (Fisanick)

Foreign Culture

Syrian Folktales (M. Imady)

The Rise and Fall of Muslim Civil Society (O. Imady)

The Secret Life of a Former Puppy: Tales of Syria (Al-Halool)

The Subversive Utopia: Louis Kahn and the Question of National Jewish Style in Jerusalem (Sakr)

Thoughts without a Title (Henderson)

Psychology & Philosophy

Anger Anonymous: The Big Book on Anger Addiction (Ortman)

Anxiety Anonymous: The Big Book on Anxiety Addiction (Ortman)

Awesome Couple Communication: Expressing What You Mean and Understanding What the Other Meant (Pickett)

Depression Anonymous: The Big Book on Depression Addiction (Ortman)

From Deep Within (Lewis)

Road Map to Power (Husain & Husain)

The Marriage Whisperer: How to Improve Your Relationship Overnight (Pickett) (IPPY Living Now Gold Medal)

Understanding the Analyst: Socionics in Everyday Life (Quinelle)

Understanding the Critic: Socionics in Everyday Life (Quinelle)

Understanding the Entrepreneur: Socionics in Everyday Life (Quinelle)

Understanding the People around You: An Introduction to Socionics (Filatova)

Understanding the Seeker: Socionics in Everyday Life (Quinelle)

Understanding the Structurist (Quinelle)

Humor

How My Cat Made Me a Better Man (Feig)(Book of the Year Finalist)

Mommy Poisoned Our House Guest (S. Leaver)

The Musings of a Carolina Yankee (Amidon)

Parenting

365 Teacher Secrets for Parents: Fun Ways to Help Your Child in Elementary School (McKinley & Trombly) [Recommended by US Review of Books; Selected as USA Best Book Finalist]

How to Be a Good Mommy When You're Sick (Graves)

I Am, You Are, My Kid Is... (Leaver)

Lessons of Labor (Aziz)

CPSIA information can be obtained
at www.ICGtesting.com
Printed in the USA
FSOW04n0355171017
39857FS